PENGUIN BOOKS

MOTHERLAND

Fern Schumer Chapman a former reporter for the
Chicago Tribune and *Forbes*, has taught at Northwestern
University's Medill School of Journalism and written
for *The Washington Post, The Wall Street Journal, Fortune,
U.S. Nerws & World Report,* and many other publications.
Visit the author's Web site at http://www.motherland.ws.

FERN SCHUMER CHAPMAN

To Jill and Henry, Share your stories, they are a family treasure.

Best,

Fern Schumer Chapman

Motherland

Beyond the Holocaust:
A Mother–Daughter Journey to
Reclaim the Past

PENGUIN BOOKS

PENGUIN BOOKS
Published by the Penguin Group
Penguin Putnam Inc., 375 Hudson Street,
New York, New York 10014, U.S.A.
Penguin Books Ltd, 27 Wrights Lane, London W8 5TZ, England
Penguin Books Australia Ltd, Ringwood, Victoria, Australia
Penguin Books Canada Ltd, 10 Alcorn Avenue,
Toronto, Ontario, Canada M4V 3B2
Penguin Books (N.Z.) Ltd, 182–190 Wairau Road,
Auckland 10, New Zealand

Penguin Books Ltd, Registered Offices:
Harmondsworth, Middlesex, England

First published in the United States of America by Viking Penguin,
a member of Penguin Putnam Inc. 2000
Published in Penguin Books 2001

5 7 9 10 8 6 4

The experiences recounted in this book are true. However, in some instances, names and
descriptive details have been altered to protect the identities of the individuals involved.

Grateful acknowledgment is made for permission to reprint "The Envelope,"
copyright © 1978 by Maxine Kumin, from *Selected Poems 1960–1990* by Maxine Kumin.
Reprinted by permission of W. W. Norton & Company, Inc.

THE LIBRARY OF CONGRESS HAS CATALOGED THE HARDCOVER EDITION AS FOLLOWS:
Chapman, Fern Schumer
Motherland / Fern Schumer Chapman.
p. cm.
ISBN 0-670-88105-8 (hc.)
ISBN 0 14 02.8623 3 (pbk.)
1. Schumer, Edith.   2. Chapman, Fern Schumer.   3. Jews—Germany—Stockstadt
am Rhein—Biography.   4. Jews—Illinois—Biography.   5. Jews, German—Illinois—
Travel—Germany.   6. Stockstadt am Rhein (Germany)—Biography.   7. Illinois—
Biography.   I. Title.
DS135.G5 S373 2000
943'.33—dc21   99-023796

Printed in the United States of America
Set in Perpetua
Designed by Kathryn Parise

For my mother

Like those old pear-shaped Russian dolls that open
at the middle to reveal another and another,
down to the pea-sized, irreducible minim,
may we carry our mothers forth in our bellies.
May we, borne onward by our daughters,
ride in the Envelope of Almost-Infinity,
that chain letter good for the next twenty-five
thousand days of their lives.

—MAXINE KUMIN

Prologue

I never thought of my mother as a Holocaust survivor. She was one of the lucky ones. She had been spared, had never faced the horrors of the Nazi death camps. Yet, when she was only twelve, she lost everything but life itself: her home, her family, her language, her loyalties, her identity.

Though she was not scarred with a number, she was a kind of survivor. Like a bewildered animal, a member of an endangered species ripped from its habitat to avoid certain extinction, she had to re-create a life outside her original landscape and context. Uprooted, displaced, and spiritually homeless, she was left alone to bear her imprisoning memory, the unresolvable grief, and the full pain of surviving.

In 1938, my grandparents sent their daughter to America, all by herself, with little more than her clothes. She traveled on the German ship *Deutschland* to Ellis Island and then by train to her new home in Chicago, where an aunt and uncle had sponsored and agreed to raise her. She was one of thousands of Jewish children from Nazi-occupied countries who became refugees, traveling to any country that would accept them—England, Sweden, Turkey, South Africa, Argentina, Canada, the United States. After 1938, most rode "Kindertransport" trains to Great Britain. Parliament had granted entry to ten thousand children between the ages of three and seventeen, once their families paid a fee of $250 each. All the children were sent without parents or families, on trains so crowded that smaller children squeezed into the luggage racks above the seats.

These young fugitives from war are called "escapees." An ironic notion, since no one escapes the grip of a homeland, the first ground etched in childhood and memory. No one evades the influence and stamp of a mother who, absent or present, imprints an identity onto her child. No one escapes the motherland. Not my mother. Not me.

Her story, and mine, is about the half-life of the Holocaust and the emotional legacy of an escapee. But there is much more. It is a complicated terrain of pain and love, expectation and disappointment, past and present. Ours is the story of the land all mothers and daughters inhabit.

Here, a daughter cannot see the whole landscape; none of us really knows our mother, or for that matter, our parents. My view was particularly narrow. My mother never wanted me to know anything of her former self, so she restricted what I knew of her present self.

What I could see is that immigration and loss had ripped a fault line in her life. Suddenly transported to a new land, my mother lost herself. Her past blurred; over time, it was buried, becoming a hidden layer of her self, a stratum of a land and a life that she tried to deny ever existed. In years of digging, I managed to excavate only bits of this; my private archeology unearthed too few pieces to construct a past. When pressed about her childhood, she offered small, detached sketches that seemed to tell someone else's story. My mother presented herself as nearly tribeless, without a history, a supporting cast, even a nickname.

This was so even though my mother's older sister had preceded her in leaving Germany. A Chicago family adopted my aunt a year before my mother arrived in Chicago; despite their geographic proximity and the profound loss that might have united them, they spoke infrequently.

Reared in separate homes, by families who made no effort to bring them together, the sisters became distant. When they talked—almost always in English—they were mindful of staying in the present. I suspect they limited their contact because each reminded the other of all that was lost. Consequently, I rarely observed my mother in the role of sister, and never saw her as someone's daughter, cousin, or niece. She was always just my mother.

Hard as she tried to forget her former life, to shed the "before," it echoed in the present. My mother was like an amputee who still feels her toes. Though she made herself into someone else, small things betrayed her. I remember her hunching over her checkbook, softly muttering math in a strange tongue—German—"*Sechs plus acht ist vierzehn.*" Sometimes, when I walked past the bathroom while she was taking a bath, I would hear her repeating, over and over, words that began with a "w": "witch, walk, work." She was trying to master its sound, to rub out the "v," the last vestige of her German accent. It was her stain.

Each time I overheard her this way, I was struck by the fact that she had another self, a full yet unimaginable life folded into her being. Strangely, it was the parts I couldn't see that had formed me. I became defined not by what I knew, but by what I didn't know.

Identity is derived from self, family, place, and past. For me, most of those elements have been unknowable and my mother has been, in many ways, unreachable. All my life, I've longed for her, for facts, a lineage, a narrative stream flowing before me, within me, and beyond me.

Motherland

Chapter 1

The plane blazes toward the breaking horizon, though my mother still isn't convinced she wants to go on this trip. Sitting next to me in the window seat, she keeps shifting uncomfortably, fidgeting with the pages of a paperback romance novel and sliding her pearl ring back and forth over the knuckles of her right ring finger. She gazes out the window at her reflection superimposed upon Magritte-like clouds, and I know she wonders whether she wants to unlock the memories of her childhood, to unleash a beast that has haunted her for half a century. She fears it may control her again, just when she was beginning to feel she controlled it. But another part of her wants to confront the past, to re-visit the Motherland, hoping that going home will free her at last.

Each of us is all the places we have been, especially the place of our childhood. My mother says she is drawn back to her place. This journey was her idea. She insisted she needed to go, I supposed, to search for meaning in her aborted past. Or maybe just to see from where she came, to complete the circle, to round out her life. In her usual taciturn manner, she simply said, after fifty-two years: "It's time."

I try to distract her by pointing out the window—past her reflection, a self-portrait on glass—to the occasional white clouds that dot the darkness beneath us. Even farther ahead is a spectacular light show featuring the dark colors of the rainbow, violet, magenta, grays, and blues. Here, where time and space are distorted, turned inside out, I'm already in a land as foreign as Oz. Like Dorothy, I hope to learn here who I always have been.

My mother finds no solace in the colors of daybreak; she says they are ominous. I tell her I find them compelling, almost magical. We sit with our shoulders brushing, uncomfortable in our polarized perceptions. We are like two dangling magnets, alternately attracting and repelling one another. Without conversation, the plane's engines ring in our ears; suddenly, they're deafening. She shudders, shaking off her anxiety, and again fixes her gaze on her own image.

The village of Stockstadt am Rhein, Germany, is an ocean and half a continent away from my home near Chicago. When my mother came to this country in 1938, the five-thousand-mile crossing on the ship took nine days, after a year-long wait to get a passport. Today, the flight will take seven and a half hours with a strong tailwind and, as she noted when she first mentioned the trip, she can accumulate frequent-flyer miles getting there. Though we made our airline reservations weeks ago, my mother got her passport photo on a rush order just a few days ago at one of those while-you-wait places.

For as long as I can remember, the village itself has been nothing more than a dot on a map, and a small one at that. In fact, it's not even on most maps, and I can hardly remember how to say its name. Stockstadt—the place where Mom was born and the place she fled. But what happened between those two events is unknown to me. If, as someone once said, facts are the individual dots in a Pointillist painting, then this canvas is nearly blank.

What I know is that Stockstadt is, was, a pastoral farming village with cobblestone streets and bicyclists crowding out the few cars. The houses resemble each other—A-framed, three-story structures built centuries ago. About two thousand people live there, or at least that was so when Mom left. Beyond that, I can't even imagine.

My mother's house is as vivid to me as a house described in a novel. Like Thornfield in *Jane Eyre*, it is almost its own character. Somehow, the house is distinct in my mother's fragile memory, more than the people she lived with. The house was a safe, unthreatening subject from her past, so we talked about its appearance and I hoarded her descriptions. Built from local stone and wood more than two hundred fifty years ago, it looks like many Tudor-styled farmhouses on German travel posters. Everything built to last—the walls that are a couple of feet thick, the slabs of stone in the cellar—solid. I know its layout and quirks, its garden and cellars, so well that I can conjure up an image in my mind of my grandmother's house. Oddly enough, I even know some details. The mattress in Mom's room, for example, was too small for the frame, so small that a child could slip through the opening and go underneath the bed to play in a dusty den.

I know little about the people who lived in the house. Mom can see the walls that surrounded her for twelve years, but she can't exactly remember what made her father smile, or the melody of his laughter.

Beyond the house, I know only a few facts. The family had helped settle the village hundreds of years earlier, before Germany was Germany. Like all of her paternal relatives, Mom was born in that house, sixty-five years ago; most of them died in that house, too. My grandparents lived in the original house with my great-grandmother, a stern guardian to my mother and her sister. They farmed the land for decades, my grandfather making his living as a wholesaler who became something of a village leader after introducing dill, for pickling, to the area as a rotation crop.

I think of the house and the farm as solid, still standing, the only continuity in the lives of my predecessors, whom I will never know. Stockstadt is the place where the memory, or at least the family name, lives on. That, I suppose, is why I left my two small sons with my husband in a suburb of Chicago and boarded this plane—to see the place, to get a sense of my past.

Turbulence rocks the plane. With each bump, color drains from Mom's cheeks. She rings for the flight attendant and asks her for a Tom Collins, the only alcoholic drink she says is palatable. Then she asks if I would like one, though she knows I'm not drinking because I'm five months pregnant.

"I had an occasional drink when I was pregnant with you," she snorts, "and it doesn't seem to have done you any harm."

I laugh to myself, thinking that Mom probably had her annual drink the evening that I was conceived. Back home, I might have teased her or taken issue, dragging out pregnancy books to prove my point. But here, I'm not about to argue. She seems to need the victory.

I ask myself what I can realistically expect from this trip. Like an explorer rummaging through the *Titanic*'s wreckage, I'm looking for clues to who was on board, who they were, how they lived and died. But my guide, the last survivor, has tried desperately to forget. She's not even sure it happened to her. "Maybe I imagined it all," she once said. "Maybe it has all been a dream."

Will there be any physical evidence of my mother's past? What can remain of the original village, which probably was bombed during the war? What could remain, even if the village had been spared? It has been a half-century since the war; places age and evolve as people do. My college town, which I recently visited after fifteen years, looked to me like a handsome woman wearing too much makeup, its dignified old buildings renovated to house the trendy stores of the nineties. In the process, the town's character was so altered that I hardly recognized it. I felt as if I were looking at my memories through rippled water or in a distorted mirror. Of course, European towns are less inclined to change than

American ones. An older friend who revisited her hometown in France after several decades reported that "no stone had been turned" during her absence.

Even so, what can remain of a family destroyed fifty-two years ago? What can remain of the people? Of, say, my grandmother, who was killed at the age of forty-three, robbed of her home and every other possession? She left nothing, maybe not even a burial site. Now my mother is the only witness I know who can testify to my grandmother's existence. My mother remembers my grandmother through the mind's eye of a child. I think of myself at twelve—seeing so much, understanding so little.

Yet the past has strange ways of inserting itself into the present. About a month ago, a relic of my grandmother's existence arrived in the mail. Some distant cousins who fled Germany for South America sent a letter that my grandmother had written to them on December 18, 1940. Scrawled above the date in old, even German script is the word "Darmstadt"—the town where my grandmother lived after her children had gone to America and my grandfather was taken to the concentration camp. In the letter, she desperately pleads for help, for someone to find a way to get her and her husband out of Germany. In a voice I will know only from this letter, she describes the anguish of being alone, of losing her entire family. "A divided life is only half a life," she wrote. "I open the door and no one is there."

My grandmother's loss became her legacy; it is now my loss, a hole in my history. As a child, I couldn't accept that I would never meet my grandparents. They existed for my mother; how could they not exist for me? To reconcile myself to their absence, I devised the absurd fantasy that they had been reincarnated in our German-shepherd dog, Queenie. It comforted me to know that Queenie's death would be bittersweet; though I would lose my beloved pet, the company of my new grandparents would console me, since they would then come to life.

But one cold, gray Thanksgiving day when I was ten years old, the dog died. My grandparents never appeared. I mourned Queenie's death with a deeper pain than my mother could ever understand.

~

The drink doesn't seem to have helped much. Usually, one drink makes my mother giddy and then sleepy, but now she seems to have plunged deeper into her reverie. I feel as if I'm sitting on a boat holding the tether to a deep-sea diver, off somewhere in the dark depths. My mother hasn't tugged in a long while; this makes me feel agitated.

Nothing seems to hold my attention. I try reading the novel I brought along—one of those best-selling sagas of three generations of women—but that's too demanding right now. I scan the pictures in a woman's magazine, just to appear occupied. But mostly, I'm fretting over my mother as if she were my child. "Where is she?" I ask myself.

Suddenly a camera flashes, and dots of light blind my eyes. After a moment, I see a man standing before us, an acquaintance of Mom's, grinning and holding a Polaroid in his hands. While waiting to board the plane at the gate, she chatted with him about her trip and introduced me to him. When he walked away, she said she knew him through one of her singles groups.

My parents, who had been married twenty-seven years, separated a year after I finished college and divorced a few years later. Unlike most es-capees who find a partner in another refugee, my mother had married an American, alienating her not only from her past but from the community of escapees as well. She would not fraternize with those who shared her immigration experience; but she never felt entirely comfortable among Americans either . . . even my father. She needed more from him than he could give. Ultimately, her insatiable needs and his boundless ambition proved incompatible in their marriage. With the divorce, she shifted some needs and expectations she had placed on my father to me.

"Sid, what did you do that for?" Mom asks suspiciously.

"For posterity," he says, pulling the tab on the Polaroid film to re-move the picture.

The flash has brought her out of her reverie like the snap of a hypno-tist's fingers. I focus on Mom's face through hot spots; she looks as if she has returned from a distant place, glassy-eyed and disoriented. Then I notice her teeth are set, her jaw is slightly unaligned, and her penetrat-ing eyes are darting around the plane. I know the expression—she looks that way sometimes when I pry about her past. It's an annoyed, defensive look, telling me I've overstepped her boundaries, and usually I back off.

"Why did that bother you?" I ask, though at home I would never have the nerve.

"I don't know," she says. "I wasn't ready for it. I guess I feel exposed."

Trying to understand my mother is like picking up a book and starting in the middle, with very few pictures for cues. All children have a narrow angle on who their parents are; after all, they come to us with a life half lived. My mother shrouded her family, her homeland, the first twelve years of her life. Then her immigration blurred and blotted out her first years in America, from the time she was twelve until she married, at twenty-four.

Even as a young child, I sensed that what had come before was as off-limits as a busy intersection. I couldn't bring myself to ask the questions that hammered at my consciousness and occasionally threatened to slip through my lips: Where did you come from? What happened to you? When was the last time you saw your parents? What was it like to say goodbye forever? How do you live each day without them?

In time, like any child of a Holocaust survivor or escapee, I learned not even to think of asking, because I couldn't be the one to inflict more pain. Looming over every conversation, every interaction, was her anguish. Her past minimized, even negated, my own emotional life. As an adolescent, I couldn't challenge her; she had suffered enough. Rebellion was a luxury—a right for other American teenagers, but not for me. From the perspective of her loss, no minor problem I might present would matter.

In fact, from the perspective of her loss, little in her past life had value; no event, no material possession, no pictures bore genuine significance. Nothing could replace her parents, her home, her sense of place. Records of her German life weren't worth keeping; she probably threw out most of her immigration papers, letters, maybe even photographs and old family recipes.

Those few things she chose to save, the only physical evidence of her past, she kept in a tattered eleven-by-fourteen-inch yellow envelope, safely tucked away on a shelf in her closet. She never told me, but somehow I always knew, that it contained all that was left of her former life. A gray dust discolored the top of the torn envelope; the address, written in neat German script with a black pen, was so faded that even if I could read German I wouldn't be able to make it out.

One day, the unanswered questions echoed fiercely in my nine-year-old mind, driving me to push a kitchen chair into my mother's bedroom and stand on it so I could reach the envelope and enter my mother's private world. In it, I found several letters from Germany, a few photographs of people I had never seen before, and a few pieces of old jewelry, including an old rose-gold ring with two tiny pearls framing a small ruby. When my mother presented it to me after the birth of my first child, I acted as if I had never seen it before. At that time, she said the ring belonged to her mother, who had sewn it into the hem of my mother's dress before she left Germany. (The Nazis confiscated all jewelry at customs, allowing Jewish refugees to leave with only 10 marks or $2.50.) On the day my son was born, I slipped it on my right ring finger, and I haven't taken it off since then.

The pictures in the envelope, I suspect, were stuffed in the bottom of her suitcase before leaving Germany. But now she would never even look at them; maybe she's forgotten they're there. For her, these pictures were not life, only details in light and shade. Without life, she didn't want details. My mother wouldn't revisit the past. Not even in an image.

Now that I think of it, my mother had little use for any pictures. She kept them hidden, never framing or displaying them, or even assembling a photo album of our family. Long stretches of my childhood passed unrecorded. A couple of pictures capture me as an infant; one as a three-year-old commissioned by my father's mother; and then a shot of me at five, documenting my first day of school. Next I am twelve, then sixteen, only one picture each; finally, I am eighteen on my high-school graduation day. There is almost as little photographic testament of my youth as there is of hers.

Pictures spark memory, but for my mother, the past was not a place to find refuge; it was a place from which she was a refugee. She was safe as long as her memory didn't drop in like an unwelcome visitor. Pictures and relics only extended an invitation.

But I was not my mother. For me, the pictures I found in the envelope offered a thrilling if sketchy tour of her place, a moment in which to glimpse her people. One, dated December 1937, is a portrait of a woman who I eventually realized was my grandmother. She looked just like my mother, with deepset brown eyes, a high forehead, leathery skin pulled tautly over high cheekbones, hollowed cheeks, a long nose with a small bump in the bridge, and full lips. Her hair, slightly frizzy and pulled in a bun, looked like the brown of tree bark.

The woman appears in another dog-eared picture I found in one of the letters. On the back of it, someone had written "9 Okt. [October in German], 1939." The woman is standing, slightly hunched, looking much older than she was in the other picture, with one hand on her ma-tronly hip, and her other arm around a girl of about ten. The little girl looks the way my mother must have as a child. But it couldn't be my mother, since the picture was taken after she had left for America. This must be someone else's little girl. A slight camera smile contrasts with the woman's dark-brown eyes, which look dazed and dispirited. Her small frame leans on the girl, as if she couldn't stand without the child's support. She looks slightly confused, somewhat forlorn; she had lost her guiding light, her sense of purpose.

For years, when no one was home, I would take down the old yellow envelope to look at that picture of my grandmother and her little friend. I imagined that the people in the pictures actually came to life when the envelope was closed. Their world burst into being when I wasn't looking. But when I opened the envelope, they snapped back into two-dimensional stillness, like a child's game of freeze-tag. Though I couldn't experience their world, the pictures took me on a kind of tour of how they lived. And, more important, the pictures gave me a way to connect with my grandmother. I would try to imagine who she was be-yond the frozen image—how the sunlight caught her eye, how the muscles in her face tightened when she was angry or loosened when she cried, how the skin on her throat folded when she looked down.

I would fantasize our life together—the times she would have read to me when I was younger, me sitting on her lap and taking in the smells that were hers only, the times when she would sing me a German folk tune and clap my small hands together to the beat of her song. As I got older, I imagined the quiet conversations we would have had over coffee, when she would tell me how she had gotten the cups we were using and laugh about things that happened fifty years ago.

I continued to sneak the envelope even after I had moved out of my mother's house. But it wasn't until after I gave birth to my first child and knew something about mothering that I finally understood the picture of my grandmother and the little girl. When her children left, my grandmother embraced another child. Like a female dog carrying a sock, she redirected the maternal instincts that would not be denied.

We have been flying for hours. Mom never touched her dinner; the cold food sat before her all night. Though the flight attendant asked several times if she was finished, Mom kept saying, "No." When I woke up this morning and smelled the cold, soupy chicken, nausea swelled beneath my tongue and in my throat. It hasn't gone away, either. All my pregnant mind can think of is the slimy, goosebumped skin covering a part of a carcass. I seal my lips to conceal my retching.

I turn my head away from Mom and her tray and instead watch a young woman across the aisle wrestle with a screaming toddler whose ears hurt from the air pressure. The child's wails make me ache for my two boys. What if one is screaming and I am not there?

I swallow hard, dissolving the lump in my throat, and hold my head still, like a horse in blinders; I don't want to see the wailing child or get another whiff of Mom's tray. My stomach churns and contracts. Finally, the flight attendant removes it so she can serve Mom breakfast. I tell her I don't want any. But now that meal sits and Mom hasn't even noticed it. My mind fixates on her cold, runny scrambled eggs, and I swallow hard to keep my stomach in check.

The plane's wings angle sharply. Through the opposite window, I see an orderly, beautiful patchwork of farmland in greens, browns, and yellows—the earth colors are far more familiar to me than those I watched like fireworks last night. A river in blue thread quilts the squares. The engines whine in a higher pitch as the plane descends and Mom shifts awkwardly in her seat.

"Did you sleep?" she asks, already knowing the answer. I turn toward her. The eggs still smell, but I try not to look at them.

"Yeah, a little. Did you?" I ask, though I know that she never even took a pillow.

"I may have dozed off for a while." She looks disheveled, defenseless, and weary from travel; her bloodshot eyes map the private roads she took during the night.

She peers through the window at the farmland below. I search her face, somehow expecting her to recognize her homeland from this bird's-eye view of five thousand feet. She knows what I am thinking. "We could be anywhere," she says, raising both eyebrows.

"It's partly cloudy and a chilly forty degrees in Frankfurt," the flight attendant's voice blares over the intercom. "Please fasten your seatbelts and prepare for landing. . . . "

Chapter 2

"Edie," a man calls from the back of the aisle, as we gather our carry-on baggage to exit the plane. The view out the airplane's porthole is of a groggy, gray dawn and a modern steel-and-concrete complex that could be the hub of any large American city.

"Edie," the man calls again. Waving a photograph, Sid says loudly, "I forgot to give this to you."

We straggle to the hangar and Sid, wishing us a good trip, hands my mother the Polaroid shot he took on the plane. She takes it without even saying, "Thank you." When she stops at the water fountain near the gate, I take the picture from her; in it, I see her character. She looks small against the airplane seat with her head falling short of the head-rest. She is petite, almost childlike, but her face looks old, eyelids loosely folded over the eyes and skin falling away from her face; her mass of long, coarse, graying hair, and her brown eyes, dark pools of sadness. She looks like a sixty-five-year-old Anne Frank.

We don't really resemble each other, but something in my face eerily mirrors hers; something in the picture, something in her belongs to me. It's hard to identify—maybe it's in the chin, which points distinctively, or the forehead, or the eyes, so dark that the pupils are almost indistinguishable, except at close range.

"I hate pictures of me," she says. "I never think of myself the way the camera sees me."

"What's wrong with this one, Mom?"

"I don't know. I just don't think that I look like this. Do I?"

I don't know what to say. "Well," I stretch the word, stalling for an answer. Then I add teasingly, "I wouldn't send it out with your holiday cards. But it makes a statement."

"I don't send out holiday cards. Here," she says, handing me the picture. "You can have the statement. I don't want it." I look at the picture again. Staring directly at the camera, her eyes follow me from every angle.

"*Guten Morgen,*" mutters a beefy, blond-haired, steely-eyed man who appears to be my mother's age. He's wearing a light-brown uniform, leaning over the customs desk, and he does not look up from his papers.

A large, age-speckled hand suddenly darts before my face and grabs the papers in my hand. Instinctively, I jump back. He barks at me in German some bureaucratic question.

Then, in English: "How long are you planning to stay?" He looks directly at me now. He'd be perfect in the SS—right out of Central Casting—with his fair complexion and imperious manner. I half expect him to snap an arm up and salute Hitler.

"One week," I tell him.

"What are you doing here?" he says with the same suspicious tone.

"Visiting."

"Visiting who?" His eyes narrow.

"I don't know who," I say, flustered, turning toward my mother. I point at her with my thumb.

"*Wir wollen zum Dorf fahren wo ich geboren war,*" my mother says in German, as if to remind him that she is one of them. Then she translates for me: "I told him that we're going to the village where I was born."

He frowns. "You speak German with an English accent," he says disapprovingly, in English.

"Which village?" He looks at me directly for an answer.

"Stuck, Stuck-stat," I stumble. "Stuck-stat on Rhein."

"Stockstadt am Rhein," he repeats smugly, correcting my pronunciation. He glares at me. Interminable seconds lapse. At last, without saying a word, he pounds my passport with his "Frankfurt, Germany" stamp and, with a cavalier wave, dismisses me.

Why, I wonder, are we putting ourselves back in the power of these people? For Germans, it seems, blond hair and blue eyes are knowable, therefore safe and trustworthy. My dark hair and eyes, like my mother's, embody our foreignness; to this functionary, we must look like all the people Germany has banned or banished. We're either guest workers or irritating reminders of what was.

No matter; he shoos us away like a couple of irksome gnats.

For me, the intriguing dream is turning on itself, edging toward a nightmare. I realize that I've never met a real German. I have an almost visceral reaction to this customs agent; even the way he speaks sends a shudder down my spine. Hasn't almost every fictional villain since World War II been characterized by that German accent?

Germans, I think, don't fit the European image of worldliness and civility; they really don't seem European at all. Germans are marked, partly by their heinous role in history, partly by their ruthlessly efficient nature.

Until now, the only Germans I've known were outcasts, Jewish refugees who were no longer really German. They came to America as outsiders, and that feeling has never really left them. My mother recently told me that even now, decades after leaving, she still feels estranged. "I am not German anymore," she said. "I am an American, but I am different."

Even in language, as the German customs agent noted, my mother is marked as an outsider. In English, she still has a trace of a German accent; in German, she has an American accent. His observation stirs resentments and raw feelings that I didn't even know I had. Unwittingly, almost through a kind of emotional osmosis, my mother has passed down so much of herself, even her rancor. This man personifies the people who shattered my mother's life, and indirectly my own.

Now I see: I've come prepared to hate.

My mother is standing behind me, next in line. I turn to read her face; maybe she's already checking the departure times for the next plane back to the States. But she hands over her papers, never looking the man in the eye, barely acknowledging him.

"I wonder where we go to get the car," she says, facing me directly to avoid eye contact with the customs agent. "I think I saw a sign over there," pointing through an archway. Without exchanging any more words with her or even asking any questions, he thumps her passport, like a judge banging a gavel.

My mother swiftly turns her back to the man and says under her breath exactly what I am thinking: "Nazi." I'm surprised, not only by what she says, but how venomously she says it. She never calls anyone names, particularly that name.

The magnets that oscillate in our relationship now abruptly swing in a new direction, attracting me to her. We are of the same mind. So often, my mother is an enigma; generally, I understand so little of what she says and does. The usual tensions between generations split us, but there is more: a greater divide separates my mother from me. Sometimes, she is simply, absolutely a stranger.

She never was like all the other moms; she wasn't even really American. But I am. Most of my friends tried to make themselves into improved editions of their American mothers, sifting through the qualities they would emulate and those they would discard. But often I defined myself in opposition to my mother, though I never let her know. I have a "She is; therefore, I'm not" mentality. She loves to clean; I hate it. I like to travel; she doesn't. She hates to cook; I love it. For her, it must have been its own alienation to have an offspring who was a foreigner. But now, in this context, we have found a commonality; we are *other* together.

"How do you know he's a Nazi?" I ask, building on our newfound bond. He's German, he's despotic, but we don't know his past crimes. Do we assume guilt from the mere fact that he's German? Or do I consider each on a case-by-case basis, dancing around the question, "What did you do in the war, Daddy?" Or maybe my question is, "What didn't you do?" at a time when passivity itself was immoral. In my mind, I'll privately try each German senior citizen I meet on this trip, though I doubt I can be a fair judge.

"I don't know," she says. "That's the trouble, you never know who's a Nazi." That's true; they don't wear uniforms anymore.

The rental-car clerk tells my mother in German that we will be driving a Rabbit.

She turns to me and says in English, "Is a Rabbit a Volkswagen?" she asks me.

"Yes," I tell her.

"No," she replies, "I don't want to drive a Volkswagen."

"That's all we have," he tells her in English.

"Nothing else?"

"We have a Mercedes." That won't do either. The only political statement my mother ever made was her refusal to own or drive a German-made car or drink German wine. There weren't many ways she could lash out or show anger toward Germans or their government. So she boycotted the few products that Germany exported to America.

I remember that, when I was in junior high school, a Jewish neighbor bought a Mercedes-Benz and occasionally parked it in front of our house. My mother would peer through the shutters, click her tongue against her teeth, and mutter something about how she wished "that traitor" would park his car in the garage.

"Our choice is between a Mercedes and a Volkswagen? That's all?" she asks, looking chagrined.

"Yes," he says, "that's it."

I weigh the options, trying to predict which car she'll choose. I figure she'll go for the Mercedes over the Volkswagen because she'll think picking the Volkswagen could be construed as a vote for Hitler. Even now.

Displeased, she begrudgingly tells him, "We'll take the Rabbit." I missed that call. Maybe her rationale is that, if she must give money to a German business, it will be as little as possible. She signs the papers, then turns to me and hands over the keys. "Here," she says, "you drive."

My mother's flat shoes drag along the cement floor of the parking garage: her footsteps sound like those of an eight-year-old who won't pick up her feet. She has slowed, stopping frequently to set down her suitcase and carry-on bag so that she can catch her breath.

"You coming?" I ask, turning around and seeing that she's fallen nearly thirty feet behind me.

"Yeah, but let's slow down a little."

"What's wrong?" I ask.

"Nothing. I can't walk that fast."

"Here, let me take one of your bags." I grab her carry-on and sling it over my shoulder along with my purse. My carry-on is hanging over my other shoulder, and I have a luggage bag in each hand. My pregnant belly is starting to block the view of my toes. Between my mother's baggage and the weight of my baby, I feel I have taken on much more than I can manage.

Slowly, I shuffle to parking space number 54. Here is our car. The Rabbit is red, with an oval license plate identifying the car as rented. It seems trivial, but this, I think, is just another German label of "otherness."

My mother twists the map, trying to find our way, while I haltingly forge along the parking-garage aisles in search of the exit. My foot dances between the pedals as I attempt to read foreign signs.

"*Ausgang*," my mother yells suddenly, as if I would understand. It sounded as if she sneezed. "*Ausgang*," she barks again, even more emphatically. Since she knows what she's saying, she feels little need to explain it to me. But I'm completely baffled.

She has always seen me as a natural extension of herself; the boundaries between us are liquid and indistinct in her mind. By virtue of biology, because I am her daughter, I should know; I am of her, and, to a larger extent, I am herself. She has never had a clear sense of separation, of where she ends and I begin; I should know what she's thinking and understand what she's saying, even if it's in German.

"What?" I ask, irritated with this ridiculous expectation. I wrestle with the car and ride the brake. The car lurches and my mother's head bobs dangerously close to the windshield. I grip the steering wheel tighter.

"*Ausgang*," she says impatiently. I brake again. Her hand grabs the dash, bracing her forehead from the glass. She gasps with exasperation. Finally, she says in a language I understand, "Exit." Her shrill, annoyed tone sets my teeth on edge. I swerve at the last second, careening onto a circular drive that ends at the cashier's booth, where an attendant waves us on.

My mother loudly rattles the map to display her aggravation and folds it into a large neat square. I have the feeling that she hasn't even found Germany yet. She could never read a map, though that never stopped her from navigating. She turns it in her hands again.

"I don't understand this," she says. "It seems like they would mark where the airport is." She clicks her tongue, tosses the map into the foot well, and directs me. "Just follow the traffic. They're all going to the Autobahn anyway."

"Yeah, but how do we know which way to go once we get there?"

"I'll know," she says, as if she knew this place like the back of her hand. Of course, none of this was here before the war. I doubt she was ever in Frankfurt as a child, though it's only forty kilometers—about twenty-five miles—from her hometown. When she lived here, Germans traveled by bike or train. She told me that most people lived and died in her village without ever going as far as the next county or even setting foot on the hills that they could see from the village. Then again, she once mentioned an uncle who lived in a nearby town and bought one of the first cars in the area. I think she said that everyone thought her family was so progressive when he'd come by to take them for a Sunday ride. Still, they couldn't have taken this route.

We find the Autobahn and my mother tells me to go in the direction of Gross-Gerau. "That's the town near mine," she says.

Mine? I'm surprised that she is taking ownership. How is it that now, after all these years of denial, the village belongs to her? Why is it okay to be here now? Why did we come? It was easy; after all, it's 1990 and anyone can go anywhere in the world. But it took my mother decades to make this decision. She had other opportunities. In fact, during the 1970s, the German government paid airfare for thousands of refugees to visit their hometowns. Unequivocally, she refused.

So what has changed? Why does she want to expose herself to the raw past? Why would she want to return to a place, to a people who murdered her parents, rejected her, stole her home? Wouldn't most people in her situation make a clean break, never to return? They would be filled with a pure and justifiable hate and stay as far away as possible.

Then again, there are all those stories about offenders returning to the scene of the crime; do victims return, too? Maybe she's more like an abused child who, no matter what pain she has suffered, still loves the abusing parent.

"Why did you come now?" I finally ask out of frustration. I didn't dare raise that question while we were planning the trip. I feared if I asked before we left she might think it over and decide she didn't really want to go after all. So we focused on the details of organizing the flight schedule and how we'd get to the airport, rather than why we were taking the trip and what we hoped to do in Germany.

"What made you decide to take this trip now?" I rephrase the question. As we clip along the highway at nearly eighty miles per hour to keep up with the flow of traffic, the fall hues—browns, yellows, and burnt oranges—streak and blur through the car windows in the morning light. It is 2:00 A.M. Chicago time, 8:00 A.M. here in Germany.

"I told you," she says emphatically. "It was time." An absence in her eyes makes me even more suspicious of her answer.

"Oh, come on, Mom. You gave me that line before." Still irked by that "*Ausgang*," I'm out of patience. "What's that supposed to mean?"

"Because," she starts, then stops.

"Because why? Why is it time?" I ask, making it clear in my urgent tone that I need a better answer.

"Because, because," she stutters nervously, and then blurts out, "they'd be dead by now anyway."

"Who?" I ask. "Who'd be dead?"

"My parents," she says. "They'd be ninety years old, and by now they would have died a natural death."

I roll her answer over in my mind. Talking to my mother can be like decoding hieroglyphics. I've learned to read meaning in her facial expressions, gestures, and few words. My mother rarely negotiates or even discusses feelings. She doesn't trust herself with deep emotion; it's too powerful, too painful. So, like many who experience trauma, she compartmentalizes her pain. She has developed a kind of fail-safe for her emotions, training herself to focus on the little things to keep her mind off larger issues. As she admitted to me recently, without a hint of self-awareness, "I never look at the big picture."

She uses minutiae as her armor. The superficial level of reality is where she's comfortable, and it's easy to understand why: She can control the waxy buildup on her kitchen floor, or fill the car's gas tank, or rub away the streaks marring her window. But she can't control her past. She clutters her mind with quotidian details, filling the bytes of her brain to capacity, to avoid what she can't bear.

When she must endure something painful, her brain short-circuits her emotions so that she seems to feel nothing. At my aunt's funeral thirteen years ago, I sat next to my mother and openly wept for a relative I didn't know well while my mother remained completely composed, distant, and stone-faced. She was mourning the passing of her last living relative from Germany, the loss of someone who had shared her childhood and immigration, her sister. Yet she was mute.

So her cryptic words now mean little to me. I don't have enough to go on. Back home, I'd give up, leave it at that. But we're here in Germany. Her homeland. Or, even if she no longer calls it that, it is the place of her childhood. She came with a purpose, though she hasn't stated it. I assume she wants to share her past, or at least talk. Therefore, it seems to me, all the rules of our relationship are suspended. I'm justified in asking a few questions. That's why *I* came here.

"So?" I look at her. "What does that mean? They would have died a natural death?"

She raises her eyebrows, surprised that I'm pursuing it, then turns away from me. I'm not giving up. I wait. Several seconds pass. I begin to think she's not going to give me an answer. Maybe I've crossed the line, maybe she came all this distance and still intends to keep the gate closed.

"Until now," she says in a low voice, as if she were talking to herself, "they were still alive for me."

"Alive?" I pursue her, thinking of how her past was an open wound; she could never mention her parents without tears glazing her eyes.

"Yes, alive," she says, turning from the window to look directly at me, "in my mind." Then, letting me see the chasm between us that is her past, she adds dry-eyed, "They lived in me."

I always sensed that. For her, the past isn't prologue; it is the whole story. The past is always present, as those she loved in Germany have dwelled in her inner life. Death ended the lives of her mother and father, but it didn't end the relationships.

Though she acted as if she had divorced her childhood, the people in her past beat within her like a second pulse. Memories and images must continually flash across her mental screen and remembered conversations constantly replay. Her mind is like a private, strangely interactive museum. Her soul is forever held hostage to another world.

She would always advise me to "put the past in the past," but now I see that she was really talking to herself. She wished it were that easy. Usually her tears came at weddings, birthdays, graduations, and other special events. At each holiday dinner table, she must have looked around for the relatives who should have been there, accounting for the missing. Any occasion was a reminder to her of who was gone.

She lived her life with an eye on the rearview mirror. Nevertheless, now they would be old, probably dead. And that has released her. They are not in full view anymore. Maybe it is finally over; she can go home again, or at least to the village she now can call "mine."

We drive in silence for several miles and I feel her draw away from me. Now I'm sorry I pushed her. I shouldn't have gotten irritated when she wouldn't give me an answer. I should have let the guilt and pity that usually control my impulses restrain me.

Maybe, on this trip, I should just let her share what she wants. Being here is hard enough; maybe I shouldn't press her with my consuming needs and unanswered questions. But I can't help myself. All my life, we've done it her way and I've come away empty and frustrated. I feel I have a right to know; her past is not hers alone. It's my past, too, my children's history. I'd like to offer this baby and my boys a context, not a black hole.

Though it's unpleasant for both of us, my persistence has paid off. I know something now that I didn't know before. Memory for most is a kind of afterlife; for my mother, it is another form of life. I try to imagine the voices she hears as her brain plays two records simultaneously, the past and the present. She has endured this eternal theater, has never even shared it—though at times she seemed withdrawn, despairing, and distant.

Her past, from my childish perspective, was ancient history. But for her, scenes from decades ago had their own immediacy. Her inner life is schizophrenically filled with both the here and now and the there and then.

"We can't leave Germany without seeing Mina," she pipes up, startling me.

"Mina?" I ask. "Who's Mina?" I've never heard the name before.

"She lived with us."

"When?"

"Here in Germany, when I was a little girl," she says, looking surprisingly animated, almost excited at the prospect.

"Who was she?" I ask.

"The maid whose family lived around the corner."

"Mom, how old would she be now?"

"I don't know. Let's see. She was maybe six years older than me."

"She was your maid?"

"Well, sort of. Her family had a lot of children and they didn't have much money. Since Mina was one of the oldest, she lived with us and did chores in exchange for room and board. But mostly we played together. She was only eight when she first came to us. So let's see." She pauses. "She's probably seventy-one now."

"Are you sure she's still alive?"

"I'm sure she is."

"How do you know?" I ask. "When was the last time you heard from her?"

"I don't know. I think she tried to help our family after I left, but I'm not sure." She pauses again, and then adds, "I don't know. Maybe I dreamed it."

"That would have been fifty years ago," I remind her.

"She sent me cards on my birthday after I came to America. Just after I had gotten married, she sent me a card that said that when I had children she hoped I would have a girl."

"That was forty-one years ago, Mom. When was the last time you heard from her?"

"Maybe just after you were born."

"That was thirty-six years ago."

"Her name is Mina . . . Wilhelmine Lautenschläger," she goes on, ignoring me. "No, no. That would be her maiden name. She married a German POW; he was an American prisoner, I think. His name was Fiedler. Yes, her married name is Wilhelmine Fiedler. I'm sure she still lives in Stockstadt."

"Then we'll ask about her when we get to the village," I say indulgently, though I doubt we'll find her. It's been nearly four decades since my mother heard from her last. "Did she have any children?" I ask.

"Yes, I think she had just one son. I remember she wrote me when he was born. She named him Jürgen and he would be about, oh, let's see, ten or twelve years older than you." I'm about to suggest that maybe we'll be able to find him when my mother announces, "You know, Mina was like a sister to me."

A sister? Her own sister never really seemed like a sister to her. Growing up, I visited my aunt's house only a handful of times. On those rare occasions, the two carefully danced around each other, with the stiltedness of two distant relatives at a family reunion. The past, their only real tie, became an elephant in the room that they ignored. That left them with little to share.

But now my mother is claiming a new sister, someone closely bound to her who shares only her German memories, someone who knew her on the other side of the fault line. In my private archeology, this is a significant discovery, the equivalent of unearthing a link between the past and the present.

Then she says exactly what I'm thinking: "We've got to find her."

Chapter 3

"Are we here?" Mom asks, as we drive into a town on what is clearly its main street—paved, not cobblestoned, framed on each side by modern storefronts, streetlights, and sidewalks.

"How would I know?" I snap before I can catch myself. I've never been here before. And I can't read the signs since they're all in German.

Distracted by her surroundings, she doesn't notice my irritation. "Could this be it?" she asks again.

Her eyes dart around the car, stabbing at each window for a recognizable site. Before us, a motorcyclist's leather jacket bristles with a dragonlike appliqué on the back. I wonder if the Hell's Angels have gone international. Out Mom's side, a health club's big neon sign flashes the jackknife moves of a bright-blue diver. Out my side, a video store displays posters for *Kojak* and *Miami Vice*.

Evidently, the town is as unfamiliar to her as it is to me. So maybe she's asking a reasonable question: Are we here? Feeling contrite and noticing that the odometer says we've traveled exactly forty kilometers from Frankfurt, I respond to her question: "I think this is it."

We pass an Aldi food store and a drugstore with a huge sign for "Toto."

"What's 'Toto'?" I ask.

"I don't know," Mom says. Then, after mulling it over, she adds, "I think it means 'Lotto.'"

She looks around again. "Are you sure this is it?" she asks incredulously. "Did you see any signs? Maybe we took a wrong turn."

"Well, this should be Stockstadt," I say, now hearing the mispronunciation that the customs agent corrected back in Frankfurt. "We're in a town right near Gross-Gerau." I stumble on that name, too. "Doesn't anything look like what you remember?"

"No," she says. "Nothing." Her gaze burns through the windshield, as if she were staring into a crystal ball waiting for some familiar image to materialize.

"It's so big," Mom says. "It's so, so"—she stops, searching for a word—"so different."

We could be anywhere. We could be in America. The town's business district, about three blocks long, has been gentrified; centuries-old buildings from which a small grocer or a shoemaker might have eked out a living are now trendy boutiques selling designer fashions and dishes. All of it looks newly done. Maybe if we had come five years earlier we could have seen and felt what was once here. But these revitalized remains seem free of memories, secrets, any history at all. Hardly a promising site for an archeological dig; no clues to my past can be hidden here.

Disappointment surges within me and I'm suddenly sorry I came. Each time I picture one of my little boys at home, I chase away the thought as if it were a neighbor's dog howling at my back door. The howl—primordial, urgent, and needy—fills me with panic, sadness, and homesickness. Occasionally, I catch myself at the edge of tears. Maybe it's exhaustion or pregnancy hormones; or maybe it's just that I've never been out of their sight for more than a few hours at a stretch. I feel so far away now, so disconnected. It seems silly when I know I'll be back with them in a week, but that doesn't take away the pull and pain of the moment.

The picture of my grandmother leaning on the strange girl is even more poignant now. How could she bear to separate from her children? How could she do it, not knowing when she would see them again? Not even knowing whether she would see them again?

"We are still hoping to get together with our children," my grandmother wrote in the winter of 1940 in the letter she sent to her relatives in South America. "No one can believe how much pain this causes.

"It is very cold," she continued, in an old German script that looks like a hard rain on a windowpane, "and I am wearing the brown, hand-knitted stockings that Oma Sara [her mother-in-law] made for my dear daughter. I am happy with them because they keep me much warmer than all the others."

As we wait at a red light, a man a little older than my mother steps down from the curb and begins crossing the street, painfully slowly, watching the ground so as not to stumble. He uses two steel hand braces to walk, because from the knee down his right leg is missing. Its empty corduroy pant leg is safety-pinned to a back pocket.

The stoplight turns green just as he lumbers in front of our car. The man glares through the windshield to be sure we've seen him and won't run him over.

"That's how you know you're in Germany," Mom says.

"How?" I ask.

"The war victims."

"German war victims?" I ask, turning toward her; somehow that dimension of the story eluded me.

"Yes, of course," she says. My mother was a victim of the war; but I had never thought about the wounded Germans and the other victims here. I study the man's uncertain gait as he struggles to the curb. This man, and all of the perpetrators, have their own stories to tell, I suppose. Maybe this man's daughter has her own emotional legacy from the war.

We drive on, and after about eight blocks, we pass out of the main business district. "That's it?" I ask.

"I guess so," Mom says. "Listen, I think we should go back to the drugstore, the one with the Toto sign, and see if there's a phone booth there. That way, we could look up the address of the Town Hall. Maybe we can get a street map, too."

"Okay." Well, I don't have any better suggestion. I feel as if we're stuck in some twilight zone, where memory, an unreliable guide, is nonetheless the only guide we have. I figured Mom would recognize something here, but for all she knows, we could be in Wisconsin. It took her so many years to work up the courage to return, and now it seems that her hometown doesn't really exist. She has suffered so powerfully from memories of this place that isn't.

This town has followed the pattern of growth, decline, and regeneration common to all populated areas. Now its shape is different, its face unrecognizable. It's as if my mother is gazing at her mother after a fifty-year absence: she has aged, no longer the woman my mother knew as her mother.

We loop back to the drugstore, park the car, and find a phone booth just inside the shop. Mom picks up the white pages of the phone book whose cover reads, in bold black print, "Stockstadt am Rhein."

"Well, this answers one question," I say, pointing at the lettering. "I guess we're in the right place."

"I knew we were in the right place," she says, "because of the lady-bugs."

"Ladybugs?"

"Yes, didn't you notice?" Actually, I had noticed that dozens of red dots landed on the windshield when we were stopped at the light, but I was preoccupied with the German war victim. "They're everywhere," she says. "And that's what I remember about Stockstadt. There were always thousands of them." So in Stockstadt whimsical ladybugs have mocked time and events. Then my mother adds, "That's the only thing that hasn't changed here."

I browse through the drugstore aisles as she looks at the phone book.

After a while, I realize that, although it should only take a few minutes to get the address, Mom's been standing there, half-glasses perched on the end of her nose, for a good ten minutes. Finally, I go see what's taking so long.

Mom's holding a piece of paper that says, "Town Hall, Rheinstrasse 1" written in her evenly slanted, loopy script. She perfected her handwriting during hours of practice at a German grammar school that, if it still exists, must be near where I'm standing. Never before have I been this close to her past.

I look over her shoulder and notice that she is scanning the "W"s in the phone book. "What are you doing?" I ask.

"Hmmmmm?" she says in the same distracted "Don't bother me now" tone she used when I was a child and had asked a question she didn't care to answer.

"Who are you looking for?" I ask again, following that childhood pattern through its familiar course: I ask; she ignores. I ask again; she either changes the subject or withdraws. Often, she terminates the exchange with, "I don't remember." On rare occasion, she weakens and responds.

She hasn't answered yet. "Who are you looking up?" I insist, watching as her finger runs down the "W-e-s"s. Westerfeld—my mother's maiden name. She is looking to see if anyone is left.

"Who might be living here?" I prod. "Who could be left?"

She looks up from her book—not at me, but in my direction. "My father," she says with a distant gaze.

I think I may never have heard her speak those two words together. For a moment, I'm stuck, trying to place who she's talking about.

"Huh? Your father? Didn't . . . Didn't he . . ." I can't bring myself to finish the sentence.

"Yes . . . At least, I think so," she says. "But I always held out hope. Somehow, I thought I'd find him here."

"Don't you think he would have contacted you if he had survived?"

"Yeah, but maybe he couldn't find me," she says dismissively. "I always thought, if anyone survived, he would." She's still skimming the tiny print, the "W-e-s"s that don't include her family.

"He was so strong," she murmurs, "I still can't believe he's gone."

Finally, she closes the phone book. "He's not here," she confides. "Not one Westerfeld is left in Stockstadt."

We get back in the car and slowly drive down the main street again.

"Do you know how to find that street where the Town Hall is?" I ask.

"I have no idea," she says.

"What was it called? Rhein, rhein?" I stammer.

"Rheinstrasse," she says. Then, to avoid another "*Ausgang*" exchange, she acquiesces, "*Strasse* is 'street.'"

"Is Rhein-whatever-it-is the name of the main street?"

"No, it's off the main street," she says. "We lived on the main street and there was only one other house on it. My cousins, the only other Jewish family in town, lived in a fancy house about a half-mile up the road."

"Could you see the Town Hall from your house?"

"Yes, it was across the street. But I can't find our house," she says, peering out the window and overlaying her remembered pictures of the past onto this busy foreign street. Then she adds, "So I can't figure out which building would be the Town Hall."

I slow the car at every intersection as we make our fourth swing down the main street. This time, I squint at the white lettering on the cement posts that look like the ones identifying streets in America's quainter suburbs.

"Rhein-strasse." Now aware of my awful pronunciation, I bumble through some bastardization of the street name. "Here it is"—making a quick right turn into a drive that leads to a large, low, modern concrete-and-glass building. A sign in front announces "Rathaus."

"Well, this is new," she says. "The Town Hall didn't look anything like this. It used to be a really beautiful old building.

"And it had a bell tower," she adds, "where a flock of storks had built a nest."

"I've never seen a real stork," I say. "I wouldn't know one if I saw one."

"They were the only storks I've ever seen—white with a dark belly. The birds made a nest in the bell tower during the summer and then they'd migrate somewhere every fall. I think they went to Africa. But every year they came back."

"I didn't know they migrate," I say, "but, come to think of it, they'd have to. To deliver babies."

"Uh-huh." She smiles. She's quiet for a moment, lost, I suppose, in the memory of the storks. Then she tells me what she's thinking: "They came back every spring. They were special to me. They were my summer pets, but I didn't have to take care of them. I could even recognize some of them and I gave them names. Each spring, when the weather would turn warm, I would wait for the storks to come back."

At last, this is what's beyond the fault line. The storks, a sweet memory of childhood, the stuff she discarded along with the rest of her past. It is her loss as well as mine. I know her so well, and yet I know so little about her.

There was a one-way window between us: she could see me, but I couldn't see much of her. Most mothers and daughters, it seems to me, observe each other in a mirror, reflecting one another at different stages of life. They are bound to each other by blood, by emotion, and by that mirror which reminds the mother of what she once was and shows the daughter what she will become. The mother relives her own childhood through her child; the daughter places herself in a context through her mother's experience.

"Which was your favorite doll?" a daughter asks to find the child in her mother. "What games did you play when you were eight?" "When did your mom let you go to the store on your own?" "When did you go out on your first date?" If I asked these questions, my mother veered off into another, less invasive topic. She changed the channel as if she were controlling the conversation with her own personal remote. Without answers, without even permission to ask those questions, and without the simple stories of childhood that most mothers tell offhandedly, I felt cut off.

Now, for the first time, she's retrieving and sharing one small piece of herself—a fragment that captures her life, her imagination as a child. She had some common childhood memories. I was never sure she did.

Her story also reminds me of my younger self. All children, I suppose, try in their own ways to grasp what's knowable about something as elusive as time. They try to find a way to measure and define it. For my mother, the magic of birds returning annually would mark spring. For me, recording dates on the bottom of drawers, toys, pages of books, and pieces of paper helped me create my own time line, a sense of my personal history. I had forgotten this childhood custom until she mentioned the storks; I'm struck by how much she and I have lost.

"Not everyone liked the birds," she continues. "Some people wanted to get rid of them. It didn't look good to have a bunch of big, dirty birds roosting on top of the Town Hall."

"Were they that dirty?" I ask.

"No, not really," she says. "They were rare and fascinating, and actually they were some help, since they ate mice."

"So what happened?"

"I don't know," she says. "When I left, the town was still fighting over the birds. I never found out what happened to them."

As I park the car, we sit for a moment. I look at the crisp blue sky and try to picture large, rangy storks with long, stout bills swooping into a long-gone bell tower. Now, in this urban setting, it seems preposterous, like pterodactyls perching on the modern office building before us.

"They must have gotten rid of the birds," my mother says bitterly. "They got rid of them after they got rid of me."

Her words sour the sweetness of the memory. No wonder she never shared this or anything else; the fault line is so deep that each story, I suspect, somehow falls into the chasm. Each memory is marred by the indelible stain of her exile.

Mom cranes her neck to look out the back windshield, straining to see across the street. When I shut off the ignition, she opens her door, gets out, and stands in one spot, slowly turning her head and shifting her feet to look around in a complete circle. As she gazes up and around, her body looks like a periscope. She must be searching for her old house.

Then she closes the car door. "I wonder if they built the new Rathaus in the same place as the old building," she says. Clearly, she hasn't seen what she's looking for. She heads toward the Town Hall's glass doors. "Let's find out."

My eyes take a few seconds to adjust to the light in the dark and dingy institutional-green hallway. Mom walks into one of the first offices with a glass door and greets, in her hesitant German, a man who is sitting behind a desk. Some of what she says I can make out, either by deduction or by the root of the words.

As she speaks, the man slowly looks up from his papers, takes off his glasses, places them on his desk, and narrows his eyes at Mom. He is a schnauzer of a man in his sixties, with a humorless face that looks as if he suffers chronically from heartburn. He rises, places his elbows on the counter between us, and says something to her in German. I think he's asking, "What is your name?"

I hardly recognize the name she gives him: "*Eh-dit Vesterfeld*," she says in German, with the "V" that stained her English.

"*Vesterfeld*." His jaw drops slightly and his penetrating eyes blister her face. Suddenly pale, as if he has seen an apparition, he surveys her intensely, running his eyes up and down her face and torso.

"*Vesterfeld?*" he says, and then he tells her something else. He goes into the back office, brings out another official, and confers with him. The second man stares at us while, I assume, the first tells him who we are. He loses color as well.

Taking direction from the second, the first man, still milky white, stands up, rubs his whiskers, lights a cigarette, and mumbles something in Mom's direction. She answers in a few words. Cigarette smoke billows toward me; I seal my lips and try not to breathe deeply to spare the baby. He then picks up the telephone, dials the rotary, and talks animatedly into the phone. The only thing I can pick up in his conversation is my mother's name.

"*Ja, ja, Vesterfeld*," he says several times. "*Vesterfeld. Ja. Nein, nein, Eh-dit. Eh-dit Vesterfeld, ja*."

"What's going on?" I ask Mom.

"I don't know," she says while watching him. "He's very hard to understand. He talks too fast. I asked him if he had any of the papers that might tell us about our family. He said something about waiting here while he finds the proper authorities."

"Who would that be?"

"I have no idea," she says.

"The proper authorities." That sounds so ominous. What a German thing to say.

After a fifteen-minute wait, a wiry, elfin-looking man in his late sixties appears in the doorway. Short and trim, with buttery white hair combed straight back, slicked against his head, and tucked behind his cupped pink ears, the man greets my mother warmly with a big, off-center smile. His ears, hair color, and quick movements make me think that if he were an animal he'd be a white rabbit.

"Hello," he says, lively dark-brown eyes dancing under high-arched eyebrows. "I am Hans Hermann, the town historian." His English is laden with a thick German accent, though he doesn't sound villainous.

"When they called me at home to tell me you were here," Hans says excitedly, "I dropped everything and came as soon as I could. It is quite thrilling for me that you came back."

"Thank you," my mother says, sounding wooden compared with Hans's enthusiasm.

So he is the proper authority. What a relief. I wonder if he served in the Wehrmacht. Probably so; I think they all did. Then my mother motions toward me and says, "This is my daughter."

"Nice to meet you," he says, extending a hand to squeeze mine heartily. "Are you staying in the hotel off the main road in Biebesheim [the next town]?"

"Yes," Mom replies.

"Ah," Hans says, "that's good."

"I'm hungry," Mom says. "Is there a place nearby where we can get something to eat?"

"Of course, let me take you there."

"What time is it anyway?" she asks. "I'm so mixed up, I don't even know if it's breakfast or lunchtime."

"Nearly eleven," Hans says. "Come. We'll go to a place that was here when you were a child."

Mom thanks the first man in German. He has kept a watchful eye on her as she talked to Hans, and he mumbles something to her as we leave.

"Did you drive around town?" Hans asks as we head outside.

"Yes."

"Things have changed, haven't they?"

"So much so," Mom says, "that I don't recognize a thing."

"Really?" he says. "I know things have changed, but there are still some familiar sites."

"Maybe I just don't remember," she says. "Though I wouldn't think I would have forgotten."

"Well, I've been here my whole life," he says. "I've seen things change slowly over the years. So maybe I've forgotten what things looked like fifty years ago."

We walk along Rheinstrasse toward the main street. I'm getting to know my way around already.

"When is your grandchild due?" Hans asks, eyeing my belly.

"In four months," she says.

"How wonderful," he says. "Is this your first?"

"No, my daughter has two boys at home."

"I don't have any yet," Hans says.

"How many children do you have?" Mom asks.

"Just one son now. He's not married," he says, adding after a moment, "My other son died just a year ago."

"I'm so sorry," Mom says. That strikes me as a deeply personal fact to volunteer upon such a brief introduction.

We walk through an old stone archway and enter a dark pub with a low ceiling that gives the restaurant a dungeonlike feeling. Shelves behind the bar display dozens of old beer steins, each different from the next. A dozen heavy oak tables that were probably here sixty years ago surround the bar; we take one in the corner.

"Were you ever here as a child?" Hans asks as he pulls out his chair.

"I don't think so," Mom says, looking around blankly. "Or maybe I was, but I don't really remember."

My mother picks up the menu and notices that the restaurant offers a familiar dish. "*Rouladen*," she says, smiling. "I have to have it. I haven't had it since I left."

I've never heard of *Rouladen* before. "What is it?" I ask.

"Oh, it's a typical German dish—pounded beef rolled up and stuffed with sausage or rice. I think it's usually baked or fried."

I wouldn't know, since my mother never cooked German foods; she left before she learned any kitchen arts. Unlike the typical immigrant who brings recipes, rituals, and songs to a new world and passes them on to the next generation, she hadn't had enough exposure to German customs. She left before the culture had formed her; the little she knew, she chose to forget. She had no desire to preserve or impart any part of Germany. "Home," Wallace Stegner once wrote, "is what you can take away with you." But she took nothing away; therefore, she was always somewhat homeless.

Her lack of heritage or traditions was most evident in the smallest ways. She never remembered any German nursery rhymes and she hadn't learned the songs of her American childhood. So I had no nursery rhymes to sing, no ethnic dishes to serve, no rituals to hand down to my children either.

After we order from the woman who owns the restaurant, Hans says, "You know, I knew your family."

"You did?" Mom looks surprised.

"Yes, I knew your older sister. She was in my class."

"Where did you live as a child?" she asks.

"In the red brick house down by the water," he says. "My family farmed and did business with your father."

She stares at him, studying his face as if it were an old picture, searching for a feature that will jog her memory. Thoughts flood my mind: they have a common experience, someone knows who she was, she has a past here, she came from some place . . . this place. Then the hairs rise on my arms as I realize that Hans knew the people in the old photographs. He is a survivor of the lost world in the yellow envelope.

When the waitress brings our food, Hans tells her something in German and then mentions the *Vesterfeld* family. She turns to Mom. I don't understand what the waitress is saying, but she picks up Mom's hand and holds it as she speaks, flashing a gentle smile between sentences.

"Did you know her?" I ask.

"No. I don't think so. But, remember, this is a very small town. Everyone knew what happened to me."

Hans starts telling Mom about some people they both knew. How many children this one had, where that one lives, what another does for a living. It's almost like a parlor game: she calls out a name she remembers and he offers a bit of the life of each. This sort of banter is exchanged at high-school reunions all the time.

I listen. None of the names are familiar, so the conversation doesn't mean much to me. Still, the whole scene is unprecedented. So much time has lapsed, but as Mom and Hans reminisce eagerly, they bridge the chasm that is my mother's past.

When I hear Mom mention Mina's name, my mind snaps back to the present. "Did you know Mina Lautenschläger? I mean, Mina Fiedler?" Suddenly, the atmosphere has changed.

"Yes," he replies, in a businesslike tone.

"Do you know where she is?"

"Not really," he says, squirming in his chair. "She was one of the only ones to leave town."

"Oh, really?" she says. "Where did she go?"

"I'm not really sure. I think she moved to the Odenwald Mountains, about an hour from here," he says and then adds, changing the subject, "Are you planning to travel outside Stockstadt?"

"I don't know. We don't have much of a plan." Then she pursues her line of questioning: "But why did Mina leave?"

"If I remember right," he says, rubbing the white stubble on his chin, "she had an asthma problem. I think she moved to the mountains for the fresh air, but I'm not really sure. She left a long time ago."

The conversation stalls, and Hans shifts uncomfortably. At last, he says awkwardly, "You know, she was an activist. During the war, she was quite outspoken."

"Mina?" Mom says. "Oh, really? I guess I knew something about that." She adds after a moment, "Because I'm not really surprised to hear it."

"After the war," he says, "she just seemed to disappear." Then, abruptly, he closes the conversation: "That's all I really know."

I'm grateful when the waitress interrupts us to clear dishes and serve coffee. When she has finished and left, Hans asks, "Well, how long are you staying?"

"A week," Mom says.

"Well, then, I'll be your tour guide for the week," he says cheerfully. "I'll take you all around. Your house, the school, the cemeteries, wherever you want to go. I'll—let's see, how do you say in English," he says with a grin, "roll, roll out the carpet. Yes?"

"Roll out the red carpet," I offer.

"*Ja, ja,* that's it. I'll roll out the red carpet."

"Thanks," Mom says, "but it's really not necessary. We can find our way."

"No, I insist," he says. "This is something I want to do." He pauses; several moments lapse, and even when he finally speaks, Hans seems distracted. "It's something I must do," he adds, not looking directly at me or my mother.

"But why?" I'm surprised to hear my own voice echo my thoughts.

"Because . . ." He pauses again, his gaze still fixed on something I can't see. "Because I owe it to your family."

Chapter 4

"Before we go see about your past," Hans says, leading us out of the restaurant and down the main street, "I want to take you to my museum."

"Museum?" Mom asks. "Stockstadt has a museum now?"

"It does, and I'm the man behind it," Hans says proudly. "It's just a few doors from here. You'll learn things about Stockstadt you never knew before."

So what, I think irritably, picturing armor, old weapons, and tapestries. That's not why I came here—to investigate the town's ancient history rather than my own story. I don't want to waste our precious week touring or doing anything unrelated to my personal dig. But I wouldn't want to insult Hans by telling him that, so I follow him and Mom into a building and then up a long staircase.

At its top, he opens the door to a room whose musty odor—a distinct smell of aging papers, mold, and dust—fills my lungs. The room, the size of my living room and kitchen, maybe thirty-two by sixteen feet, is cluttered wall-to-wall with the stuff of flea markets.

The scene looks like a page from my children's *I Spy* book, in which the viewer must scrutinize a densely detailed photograph to find various prizes. Here, a jumble of old farm tools, horse shackles, animal tusks, shields, harpoons, maps, and old clocks hangs along the walls. Pottery, gems, arrowheads, fossils, animal bones—even a skeleton—fill the shelves and cases. Thousands of things are scattered everywhere, some of value, some not; here, any relic seems worth saving. The museum looks like one of those antique shops in the city where there's so much stuff, there's barely a clear path to view the merchandise.

"Did you collect all this?" I ask.

"Why, yes," he says. "Come in." Hans is walking toward the light switch on the other side of the room. He navigates around the displays quickly and confidently, the way I find the bathroom at home in the middle of the night. "There's so much here. I've been collecting things my whole life, and about five years ago, I decided to display them in my own museum."

Hans seems to be the self-appointed curator of what looks like junk—though to him it's valuable. "You learn from old things," he says. My mother wouldn't want things from her childhood; like old pictures, they would be painful souvenirs. Even though her new possessions lack real value because they are without history, they still give her a sense of security and continuity, an impression of re-creating a home. She can't bring herself to throw those things out. She hates to make changes.

She resists even small changes, since they echo the most devastating transformation of her life. Fifty years ago, unable to exert any control over her circumstances, she simply suffered the storm that rolled through her young life. She, like many escapees, recognized that she was powerless; nothing she did would change her fate. Consequently, she learned to do nothing. Under any circumstances.

Survivors, on the other hand, were generally older than escapees and had slightly more control over their fates. They relied upon qualities within themselves that saved their lives. Torture, abuse, and loss taught survivors to be cunning, enduring, or even complicit—anything to live another day. But escapees were children and, therefore, pure victims.

Despite and because of all this, my mother's home offers her comfort, constancy, and some security. In fact, the idea of home is central to her life. She clings to the house she has lived in since I was twelve years old, a house I am sure she will live in until she dies. She can't move. This is the place that finally feels like home. It took decades to imbue it with that feeling.

Years ago, when my parents were ending their marriage, there was no question of who would get the house and its contents. Even in the heat of divorce, my father understood that his leaving my mother was devastating to her; stripping her of her home, after her childhood, would have been a cruelty he could not inflict on her, and certainly one she couldn't endure.

After he moved out, she rarely made changes, never rearranging furniture or rehanging a picture. Years after their separation, the house remains almost exactly as it was the day he left. She has created an eternal present; anything else was too frightening.

But her adherence to the status quo made me feel claustrophobic. I urged her to make some changes, any changes. Think of moving, I'd suggest. Start life over. Freshen up the house. Or cut your hair. (She has worn it in the same style for most of her life.) I wanted her to be creative, to reinvent some bit of herself; but how could she do that without a strong sense of her original self? She bristled whenever I proposed these ideas; they were far too disruptive to consider, much less carry out.

Once, out of curiosity, or maybe just to challenge her rigidity, I removed a picture from the wall. A thick, dark, accusing shadow outlined the place where it had hung. The shadow—the mark of her emptiness, her destituteness, her loneliness—made me feel as if I had bared my mother's soul. I quickly put the picture back in its place.

My mother's house is so much a part of her now that she hates being away. She becomes agitated for weeks before going on a short vacation. Her uneasiness over leaving became so intense that, several times, she backed out of traveling to Europe with my father. Months before the trip, she would plan to go but she would worry. By the night before the flight, her tension escalated into unmanageable dread, and, finally, she would tell my father abruptly, "I just don't feel I can go now."

My mother will travel if it's absolutely necessary, as when a South American relative, whom she sees rarely, stops over in a nearby city. During such a trip, she generally counts the days until she's home again; I often think of her emotional state as that of a fish flopping around desperately outside its bowl. Upon her return, when others would say, "I had a wonderful time," she always announces, "I'm glad that's behind me."

Given all this, as well as her reservations about Germany, I doubted she would actually go on this trip. Until the last minute, I expected her to find some excuse.

And I might not have minded; I have picked up some of my mother's reluctance to venture from the safety of home, especially now that I have small children. But long before I became a mother, I had absorbed her insecurities. This was apparent by the time I was four years old. When we visited anyone's house, I would refuse to take off my coat. Once, my paternal grandmother asked why. "I'm afraid that my parents will leave without me," I told her, clutching the front of my little red princess-line coat, "and I won't have time to put on my coat and catch up with them."

During this trip to Germany, my mother wouldn't have to take off her coat. With me along, she seemed comfortable and secure. By bringing me, she was avoiding a huge strain that upsets her daily life: she would have a week when she wouldn't have to say goodbye to me.

Every time she leaves someone she loves, even if she's only going to the store for a gallon of milk, she acts as if she'll never see the other person again. She prolongs each parting, sometimes as long as twenty minutes, before dragging herself out the door. It's always a subliminal minidrama reverberating the painful separation of her and her parents.

On this trip, she was taking along what she needed. I would be with her.

~

"Why do you keep all this stuff?" I ask Hans.

"The world changes; witnesses die; things perish," he says, as if he were reciting a prepared speech to guide visitors through the museum. "Except here. This is one of the only places to see the past."

I walk into the room and immediately have the sense that someone is watching me. I look around, then up. Standing over me is a mannequin wearing a Nazi uniform and carrying a rifle. His young face has a determined look, chin up, with intensely focused clear blue eyes and straight blond hair neatly combed beneath his cap. He's so lifelike that I expect him to move. I stare at his chest to see if he breathes, if he's a mime posing as a statue. Hans went to some trouble to get the right Aryan mannequin; I wonder if he took measurements, the way the Nazis did.

"Where do we begin?" Mom asks. "There's so much to see."

"Over here," he calls to us from the other side of the room. "I'm especially proud of some of these animal remains."

"I guess we're going to begin at the very beginning," I tell Mom, as we make our way toward the beginning of time.

After just a few steps, Mom stops suddenly to look at something on a shelf. "Ohhhhh," I mutter, bumping into her with my belly. "Sorry."

She's inspecting some sort of appliance: it looks like a mill or something. It has a wooden base with a drawer to catch grounds, an iron body, and a wooden handle on the side to operate the grinder.

"What's that, Mom?"

"I'm not sure if it's a grinder for coffee or pepper." She continues to examine it. "But it looks so familiar to me. Like something we used in our house."

"Really?"

"Ladies," Hans calls, interrupting us. "I'd like to show you some things over here which you shouldn't miss." He's standing next to some huge prehistoric bones, his flat palm pointing at the display shelf. Each bone is nearly a yard long and looks so heavy that I doubt I could lift one.

"These are mammoth leg bones dating from the Ice Age, five hundred thousand years ago," he says, pointing to them with pride. "They were found in Messel, a town not too far from here."

"Everything you see here came from this area," Hans continues. "We have found bones from oxen, bears, bison, rams, rhinoceros, hippopotamuses, wild horses, reindeer, and ahhh, how do you say it in English? Oh, you know, the laughing animal."

"Hyenas?" Mom asks. I listen distractedly, noticing a human skull on a shelf next to the animal bones. I pick it up and turn it in my hands as Hans continues talking.

"Yes," he goes on, "hyenas. They all once lived in the area."

I discover a large hole in the right temple of the skull. About a half-inch in diameter, it looks as if it could be from a bullet. "What's this?" I ask Hans, pointing to the hole.

"Over here, in this glass case"—he turns away from me and continues his canned presentation—"we have found dozens of iron pieces in the Stockstadt region dating back to 400 B.C."

"Excuse me," I interrupt and show Hans the hole in the temple. "Is this a bullet hole?"

"Yes, I suppose so." Hans walks over to the display case and pushes a squared-off index finger against the glass.

"Who was he?" I ask.

"I don't know," he mumbles. "Someone from World War II."

"Where did you find the skull?" I persist. The tip of his finger, underneath the nail, turns completely white from the pressure.

"In Stockstadt, by the Rhein"—dismissing the question briskly. "Here, you'll see several knives, a spear, a feather cutter, a stake, and a file used to sharpen objects. Most of what's here was found in the Odenwalds, the mountains nearby in the Rhein Main Neckartal area."

"How long ago?"

"Sorry?" he says. "How long ago did we find these items? Ohhh, they're from different periods in . . ."

"No," I jump in again. "When did you find this skull?"

"Oh, about a year ago," he says. That's how recent the war is here. Germans are still uncovering remains in their soil. Bullets and bones linger in the soccer fields where children play or in the rivers where families swim; it's as if the Americans bombed yesterday. Maybe mothers here worry about undetonated bombs or land mines. It's all so fresh.

Hans continues his tour as I return the skull to where I found it. "As you can see," he says, "this place tells the history of Stockstadt. It brings the past together," he adds proudly.

"Originally," he explains, "we had the museum in the old Rathaus. But there wasn't enough room there. After we collected more items, the museum outgrew the small space in the new building, so we moved to this location."

"Oh, that reminds me." Mom turns to him intently. "Did the town build the new Rathaus where the old one stood?"

"No, but it's not far from the original location," he answers.

"Then tell me, Hans," she goes on, "do you remember the storks' nest?"

"Of course I do."

"Did you try to save it?"

"Oh, I wish I could have," he says. "I try to get everything I can of local history, and that certainly was a part of the town as it was. When they were about to tear down the old Rathaus, I tried to move the nest. But there was no way to do it. Each time I touched it, it fell apart."

"What happened to the storks?" Mom asks. "Did they ever come back to Stockstadt?"

"Actually, the storks came looking for the nest after the new building was built," he says. "For a few days every spring, the birds would come and circle the building, probably looking to rebuild their nest. But after a while, they never came back."

The phone rings in the office across the hall. "Excuse me, please, just for a moment." Hans scurries out of the room and I can hear him talking in a loud voice in German. Mom makes her way back to the archaic kitchen gadgets.

"We used to use this kind of iron in our house," she says. "You put the hot coals in the bottom of it. Funny, I hadn't thought of that since I left here."

Yet here are reminders of that time in a small and most particular way—the household equipment that surrounded her during those days. Back then, she probably never gave any of it a thought; it was all part of the world as she had come to know it.

"Now let me direct your attention over here," Hans says as he marches back into the room and over to a gem case.

"Just a minute," Mom says, hovering over some sort of stove, the size of a hot plate. "My father used that kind of stove on the special holidays to make . . ."

"Have you seen these gems?" Hans interrupts. "They are really quite special."

Mom joins Hans on the other side of the museum, and I loiter at the household display wondering what they used the stove for. It isn't big enough for a large pot. Stumped, I join them on the other side of the room.

"Over here, you see, is our collection of precious stones—diamonds, topaz, granite, amethyst, aquamarine. It takes nature millions of years to produce these minerals and crystals.

"Over here is one of my favorite exhibits," he says as he directs us down another aisle to a case filled with World War I relics. "This exhibit is emotional for the older generation, who lived through the time."

The phone in the office rings again, and Hans excuses himself. "I'm waiting for an important call," he says apologetically as he leaves the room.

Posters, helmets, gas masks, handkerchiefs, bayonets, sabers, some sort of two-way radio fill the case. "My father served in World War I," my mother says.

"I didn't know that."

"Yes, he got some sort of citation from the government for being wounded in the war. He received an iron cross that was on a shelf in our living room. He may have even gotten some money for compensation, too."

"Really?"

"I think that one reason my parents didn't leave Germany," she says, "was because of my father's role in the war. I think he felt safe because he had served in World War I."

"But he must have seen what was happening around him," I say.

"I suppose he did, but for a long time, the men who fought in World War I weren't treated like the other Jews. They were special, so my father felt safe. He couldn't believe that the Germans he fought with would hurt one of their own."

"When things got worse, didn't he see that the family was in danger?"

"He saw, but he didn't really believe it," she explains. "Our family had lived in the town since the 1700s. There were only two Jewish families, and we didn't see ourselves as different from our neighbors." She mulls that over and then adds a line she probably heard as a child: "We didn't even think of ourselves as Jews: we were all good Germans."

A few moments pass as she obviously replays old scenes and conversations. "There was another problem, too," she continues. "My grandmother, my father's mother, refused to leave."

It is as if she's reporting a debate she can still hear. I picture my mother as she is now—gray, pale, slightly slouched, aged hands folded in her lap—quietly sitting in the corner of her parents' living room, still listening to the grown-ups discuss what they should do. "Oma Sara would always say, 'I was born a German and I will die a German.' And my father would always tell her, 'Well, I can't go without you.'"

"So when did they finally think of going?" I ask. I know from my grandmother's letter that their passports were in order on November 11, 1939, but by then they didn't have money to pay for the exit papers and passage.

"I am wishing for a way out," she wrote in the letter I have read so many times that I know it word for word. "I have written so many begging letters. If all the relatives got together, maybe we'd have enough money to leave. Have all our dear ones read this letter. If at all possible, let them help us."

"When did they realize they had to get out?" I ask again.

"I don't know. My father started to feel uncomfortable around 1935," she says. "Then my teacher came to our house to tell him that I had to go to school on Saturdays, the Sabbath. The teacher said, 'She must come. She must conform.'"

"Did you start going?"

"I don't think so."

She walks toward the kitchen exhibit again, slowly taking in the household items on the shelves and farm tools hanging on the wall—a hand weeder, a heavy skillet and cover, a washstand with a basin and pitcher, an oil lamp, some ceramic water jugs and misshapen glass bottles. Finally, she stops, standing before the small hot plate.

"Oh, what were you saying before?" I ask. "What did you use the stove for?"

"For spirits . . . to distill alcohol for the High Holidays."

"I couldn't figure that out," I say. "The stove is so small."

"You didn't need a lot," she says. "One flask goes a long way.

"Look at that butter stamp," she continues. A long metal instrument hangs high on a hook on the wall. It has a stamp on the end that looks as if it could brand a cow.

"We had one just like that," she says. "My mother was very proud of her butter. She said she knew how to make it creamier than anyone else, and she would give some to the neighbors. She always used that kind of press to show it was hers."

I squint at the end of the butter press to make out the initial it imprints, but it's high on the wall and it hangs at a funny angle. I dance on my toes and lift my head to examine it. "Mom," I say, "look at it. The butter press looks like it stamps a 'W.' "

"No," she says. "It couldn't be. Really?"

"Well, I can't say for sure, but it looks like one to me. See for yourself." It's hard to tell, since the press is so flattened and worn from use.

I move out of the way so that she can stand in my spot and get the best view. After straining on her toes for a minute, she says, "I can't make it out."

We move on to a glass display case from which our reflected faces peer back at us, mine almost a head above hers. My body is that of my mother's distorted into the shape of a bowling pin. While looking at our reflections, I'm startled to glimpse, out of the corner of my eye, my grandmother. My mother's face echoes my grandmother's as she looks in the photograph in the yellow envelope. That makes me the unknown little girl in the picture. The glass reflects a bizarre family portrait, images cut and pasted onto each other. A postmodern picture no one can see but me.

"I had a school satchel just like that," Mom says, cupping her eyes to see what's in the display case. I press up against the glass to inspect the old, worn greenish-brown leather saddlebag surrounded by old school supplies: a compass; a wooden ruler that no longer gives a measure, only splinters; pens and chipped inkwells discolored with flaking, dried black ink.

"It had a fixed strap just like that one. And it wasn't evenly sewn, just like that." She points at the exhibit. "My initials were on the strap."

I feel hot and then cold as she walks around the case and adjusts her glasses to get another angle on the strap. "Come here, I can't make this out too well." I follow her, and our reflections shuffle around the corner with us. I push my nose against the case. Something is branded on the strap about an inch above the stitching, some faded initials hand-tooled into the leather. I can't make out their shape, but a shudder takes hold of me, shimmying down my spine.

"Maybe it's yours," I say, rubbing my cold hands together. "Could that be?"

"I don't know," she says, squinting behind her glasses for a sharper focus. "I suppose it's possible."

Her casual phrasing in no way addresses the feeling here, hers and mine. I suspect it's her way of distancing herself from a reality that is too chilling to capture in conversation.

She expected to come back and see her house, the Town Hall, and some people from the past. But she didn't expect to find her mother's butter press or her old school bag. They drove her away, but kept her things. Are they in this museum now because it is too distasteful for those who had her family's things to live with them and the memory of how they got them?

Whatever the reason, it's as if she herself is only one step removed from being on exhibit.

"What do you think happened to all your old stuff?"

"I have no idea." She turns away from the case. "I remember I got a letter from my mother saying that people had thrown stones and bricks through the windows in the middle of the night on Kristallnacht"—the

Night of Broken Glass. "She said that the men stole many things—the linens, the dishes, the silver, even some of her clothes."

Suddenly, I shift uncomfortably, looking away from Mom to cue her that Hans is standing behind her. I don't know how long he's been there.

"Are you talking about Kristallnacht?" he asks in a heavy, solemn voice.

"Yes," my mother says, slightly startled. Then she bites her lip. Each of us looks from one to the other, the subject of Kristallnacht dropping a tense fog over and between us. Hans's eyes narrow, as if he's looking inside himself for guidance. He seems conflicted, uneasy that we are facing a subject he had hoped to keep as distant as France.

I've read that Germans are nothing like Americans when confronting their role in the war and their collective guilt. After Vietnam, Americans wrote books, produced movies and talk shows, and endlessly discussed the war, as if they were purging themselves through a sort of public confessional. But for years, Germans wrestled privately with their culpability; they didn't talk about it much. They acknowledged the Third Reich tacitly, mostly through their rejection of it. For a long time, they avoided militaristic or Nazi-evoking images. Even the uniforms made the military look more like businessmen than soldiers. And by the 1970s, German officers hated to wear uniforms in their private lives.

Amity Shlaes explains in her book, *Germany, The Empire Within*, that the German public image changed somewhat in 1985, when President Reagan paid an official visit to a cemetery where soldiers and some SS were buried. Before Reagan went to the Bitburg cemetery, the American press argued that his visit would be a salute to the men who had served Hitler. However, the Germans claimed Reagan's visit was a statement to the world that Germany's war dead should be honored; they should be recognized as soldiers rather than disgraced conspirators.

Still, until recently, most Germans of my mother's generation have been simply silent. Having offered to be our guide, Hans can no longer ignore the past. Our presence confronts Hans with himself and his country, forcing him to look again at things that happened fifty years ago. He must navigate his way through an internal, introspective maze. I sense his ambivalence; a part of him seeks catharsis, but another part wants to share with us only the Germany he loves, overlooking its ugliness.

Now I see that this museum visit resounds with the same question that has tormented my mother her whole life: How does one live with the past? Here, how do Germans live with their own silence, the shame and the guilt that shadow their lives? What stories do they tell themselves to rationalize their behavior so that they can go on?

Awkwardly, I redirect the conversation: "How did you get all this stuff?"

"What do you mean?" he asks.

"All these kitchen items and farm tools," I say. "Where did they come from?"

"When I decided to assemble the collection," he says, "people put things in a box outside the museum's door. I asked for information about each piece, but many people left things without filling out the forms. So I don't know much about some of these items."

Then Hans puts up a hand suggesting he has something else to say and he doesn't want to be interrupted. He looks as if he's giving sworn testimony by raising his right hand. "About Kristallnacht, you should know," he says slowly, "no one from Stockstadt participated in Kristallnacht. The Nazis came in cars from other towns. They were not local people."

Huh, I think nastily. If nobody from Stockstadt looted on Kristallnacht, then how did these objects, which probably belonged to my mother's family, come to these shelves? Those other Germans, the ones who didn't throw rocks—did they stand around and watch? Did they take my family's things? Who *did* throw the rocks?

"Then who were the people in the cars?" I ask, careful not to snap.

"I don't know. I didn't know them," he says, distancing himself from the Nazis who perpetrated Kristallnacht and, I suppose, trying to find a comfortable way to be a German. Ironically, the Germans' ostracism of the Jews brought the Germans the ultimate ostracism: they can no longer take pride in their nationality, in who they are. "We all thought we were good Germans," my mother had said, and she spoke for a nation. Yet being a "good German" led, of course, to Nazism. Then there were no more "good Germans," since most committed or complied with pure evil. And there's really no way to distinguish the true collaborators from the coerced conformists.

For the first time, I see in Hans how the Nazi era has been internalized by Germans as individuals. Even when Germans aren't judged by other Germans, they must be judged by their own consciences. Most German perpetrators were never punished or rewarded for their behavior, but they had learned something about themselves. They know what they did or didn't do in the most morally fraught moment of their lives. They have seen themselves in extreme circumstances and, in that, they have seen their own extremes. They have lived with that personal knowledge, that guilt or pride, these fifty long years.

Nazism, I suddenly think, is a mirror, the distorting kind of wavy glass in which an image may be less attractive—or more so—than in reality. Once Germans have seen their reflection, it is all they know of themselves.

Most of us never have to look in that mirror.

Chapter 5

*J*et-lagged into a stupor, I'm sitting in the small lobby of our hotel, waiting for Mom to get our room key, when a mother pushing her toddler in a stroller accidentally bangs the glass entrance door. The mother struggles, trying to open the door while maneuvering the stroller over the threshold. I get up and hold the door for her. She prattles to her son in that high-pitched tone reserved for little children, smiling at me as she enters the lobby and adding in an adult voice, "*Danke.*"

My eyes fall to the curly-blond-haired, brown-eyed child, his face, round and soft, and his skin, pink and clean. I marvel at his apple cheeks, round as my younger son's; his ears, mother-of-pearl seashells; his button nose, the nostrils, tiny caves; impossibly long, dark feathery lashes—the kind only a child has—fringing clear yet dreamy eyes.

Not even a work of art could capture such perfection. The stone in my throat sinks to my heart.

"Okay," Mom says, holding up a key chain. "We're all set. We go up those stairs." I grab for my suitcase handle, but keep my eyes on the child, drinking in his sweetness. He stares up at me with penetrating eyes; my stomach turns as I break the gaze.

"Mama," the child says, just as I'm about to climb the first step. His call lassos me. I freeze, overwhelmed by the same sensation I knew years ago, on my first outing alone, a couple of weeks after my first son was born. I felt as if I'd left a limb at home when, just to get a break, I went to the grocery store. While there, I heard an infant's imploring cry from several aisles over. At once, milk soaked my shirt.

A double bed crowds into the corners of this tiny room, leaving no space for a nightstand, a dresser, a luggage rack—any of the amenities most hotels offer. The bed is made in a way that, until very recently, I'd seen only in my mother's house, without a bedspread or even a top sheet. Instead, the blanket has a white lacy cotton coverlet, sort of a giant pillow sham with a hole in the center to insert the blanket. Catalogues from the finer department stores now advertise these as duvettes in designer colors and signatures. But when I was a child, no American store sold them; my mother had to sew the sheets together and trim the hole with rickrack. To me, it offered a womb: I would crawl into the hole and hide in the cave.

"This is it?" I ask Mom, since she made the arrangements. In other words, we're both sleeping in this bed?

"Yes." I dump my suitcase on what will be my side of the bed and unzip it to search for a nightgown as my mother goes to the bathroom. Exhausted from the day and the trip, we are both eager to get some sleep, though I hadn't expected to have to share a bed, especially now that I'm pregnant.

After brushing my teeth, I climb into my side and turn so that my back is toward Mom. She's lying on her stomach, curled toward me, near the bed's fifty-yard line, still awake. I hover on the cold edge, somewhere around the fifteen-yard line, teetering and then swinging a hand on the floor to catch myself just before I tumble.

When I was a little girl, Mom never liked sleeping alone. Whenever my dad would go out of town, she always invited me into her bed. Then it was a thrill to be in the warm, snugly secure place of her hugs. Now in her bed I feel uncomfortable, claustrophobic, captured. I belong to her, to her universe; the bed becomes an arena, a scene of struggle from which I can't escape. Like childhood itself.

"I . . . I can't imagine what I did," she says softly, tentatively, and then pauses.

"Hmmm?" I say, feigning sleepiness, because I'm not sure I want her to finish her sentence.

"I can't imagine what I did to make you feel my past," she says, in a low voice I am unaccustomed to. Taking this as a statement rather than a question, I elect not to answer her.

I wouldn't know how or where to begin. The past is a presence between us. In all my mother does and says, the past continually discloses itself in the smallest ways. She sees it directly; I see its shadow. Still, it pulses in my fingertips, feeds on my consciousness. It is a backdrop for each act, each drama of our lives. I have absorbed a sense of what she has suffered, what she has lost, even what her mother endured and handed down. It is my emotional gene map.

A story she told me last Mother's Day revealed that my mother had the same legacy from her own mother. That day, I seized the opportunity to ask a few questions about my grandmother, for whom I am named and of whom I know almost nothing.

"She was a very soft woman," she said. "I think I'm more like her than my father, who was stern. My mother was very giving and sensitive."

I pressed her for more details. Her eyes clouded, and then she shared one of the few stories I know about her mother. It was the only time I can remember that she told me a story about the past without measuring words and censoring meaning.

"The year before I left for America," she said, "the Nazis put more pressure on the Jews and on our family. My mother became more and more upset. One day, my grandmother, Oma Sara, told me, 'For the next few days, follow your mother around. Don't let her out of your sight.' I think my mother must have threatened suicide, and since I was the youngest and had fewer responsibilities than anyone else, I could stay close to her.

"The first day, I watched her carefully, but then—then the next day—I became bored and paid less attention to her. On the third day, while I was playing near her in the garden, she disappeared on me. When I realized she was gone, I was frantic. I searched the whole house and the yard. But I couldn't find her anywhere.

"Finally, I went up to the attic, the only place I hadn't looked. There, we dried flowers, herbs, and sausages, and kept things we couldn't keep in the house and things handed down from generation to generation; I had only gone into the attic a few times. I found her there. She was mumbling to herself and adjusting a rope over a rafter; it dangled next to the large brown sausages she had prepared for the winter.

"When she saw me, she became very irritated and said, 'Don't follow me.' I asked her what she was doing. 'Go away,' she told me, but I said, 'No.' That took a lot of courage, because I wasn't allowed to say no to my mother. I just sat on an old wooden table and refused to leave. 'I'm staying with you,' I told her. 'I'm not going downstairs without you. I can't leave you.' Then she sat next to me on the table and cried into the skirt of her dress."

I have seen my mother in the attic, too. When I was five, just after I started kindergarten, my mother got sick. My father's mother came to stay with us to give my mother the rest she needed. Mom would spend most of the day in bed, and I was allowed two scheduled visits—at lunch, when I came home from my half day of school, and late afternoon, just before dinner. When I entered her stuffy room, darkened by heavy drawn draperies, she appeared shadowy and gray in the bed.

"Do you feel better today?" I'd ask.

"About the same," she'd say in a monotone that didn't sound anything like the voice that directed my days. She looked too young to be so sick in bed. I could hear the children on the block shouting and screeching as they played on the next-door neighbor's patio.

"What hurts?" I'd ask, though it seemed like a question she should ask me, not one I should have to ask her.

"Nothing in particular," she would tell me. "But nothing feels right."

My grandmother never let me stay too long. "Come on, now, honey," she'd say, pushing open the door and poking her head in, "Mother needs her rest." Now I see that my first steps toward independence became a loss for my mother that consumed her self and took her to the darkest edge of being.

I'd leave her bedroom and then ask my grandmother when Mom would feel better. "Give her time," she'd say. But it seemed so long, in that sluggish way that hours and days pass for a child. She was getting worse. I judged her health by how long I was allowed to visit: the longer the better. But the visits were cut shorter and shorter. Then one day, I wasn't allowed into her room.

I begged my grandmother to reconsider, refusing to eat the lunch—an egg-salad sandwich, a plum, a glass of milk—she placed before me until she let me see my mother. "Please let me go in," I said. "I'll make her feel better."

The plum was among the last of a huge crop that a tree in the back-yard had produced. What started as a delightful harvest turned into an avalanche, a burden of abundance. That summer, my mother, driving herself to use every piece of fruit, spent most afternoons toiling at the stove to preserve the perishable plums. She would make pies, cakes, preserves, jam, sauce, pudding, and even soup with the hundred pounds of fruit from the one tree.

One day, I stood on a chair next to the stove and saw a nylon stocking filled with plums soaking in a boiling pot of purplish-black water. It looked as incongruent to me as Santa Claus wearing ballet slippers in one of those cartoons that challenges a child to spot what's wrong with this picture.

"What are you doing?" I asked, incredulously.

"Making jam," she said. "This is how my mother did it." The word seemed to get caught in her throat and come out muffled. It was the first time she had mentioned her mother to me.

"Who?" I asked.

"My mother," she said again, more clearly. Still, the word "mother" sounded odd coming from her. Until that moment, it never occurred to me that she actually had a mother. Why would it, since I never heard anything about her?

That summer, we ate plums, and more plums, and more plums. Jam with breakfast. Pudding for lunch. Plum butter on bread for dinner. Three and four times a day, day after day, I'd eat plums. I ate so many that I got sick of them; to this day, I won't eat one.

Now, as I looked at the lunch before me, the plum on my plate seemed larger and a deeper purple than those I'd eaten all summer. As I stared at it, sickened by its bruised color, someone banged on the door. I suddenly heard a shriek, a shrill so piercing and terrifying that my body froze; this is the scream that would come from the woman in the Munch painting. My mother came running out of her bedroom with her white terry-cloth bathrobe half wrapped around her naked body. She looked so different, so strange, that I wasn't sure that this woman was my mother. Mom was modest, rarely allowing anyone to see her unless she was fully clothed. She always wore slippers that flapped with a swift, purposeful clip. Her scream vibrated my eardrums, rattled my bones, unsettled my being.

"He's coming," she said, in a raspy, unfamiliar voice. "He's coming. He's going to get me."

My grandmother ran to her and tried to calm her down. "Who, dear? No, no," she said, in the same soothing voice she had used with me the night before, when I had a nightmare. "No one's here. You're safe here."

But my mother grabbed my forearm, frantically jerking me from my chair as my lunch plate spun to the floor. Queenie, the dog, came running and wolfed down the sandwich, then swallowed the huge plum whole, seed and all. My mother pulled me from the kitchen to the living room, toward the back door, to escape whoever she thought was coming through the front door.

"No," my grandmother kept insisting. "Edith! It's nothing. Come lie down."

I started to cry; she frightened me. Terror filled every cell of her body. Her breathing was labored; her nostrils were flared, eyes wide and deep. My grandmother wrestled with her, but she was like a wild, tormented animal, arms and legs flailing, her robe flying open to unveil her breasts.

"He's coming!" she screamed.

Finally, I asked, "Who?"

She knelt down to my level. Her pupils had dilated into flat black saucers, as if two black holes had taken over her brown irises and left nothing of the soft brown eyes that danced when I drew a picture of her and me standing under a rainbow. Her terrified focus was directly on me, went through me.

"Hitler," she howled. The word echoed in the small room, as though she were calling out from a deep, dark cave. Then she collapsed to the floor and hugged her knees, heaving uncontrollable sobs. She rocked with her arms clasped around her knees as my grandmother bent down next to her and tried to coax her back into her bedroom.

"Come, now," my grandmother said softly. "Everything is all right. Let's get back into bed."

"Who?" I kept asking. "Who's coming?" But no one answered me. I pulled back the heavy beige curtain framing the window next to the front door and saw a florist delivery man walking to his truck; he had left a box tied with a red ribbon on the front stoop.

Finally, my grandmother slowly helped my mother up, supporting her elbow. I watched them go. She walked oddly without any shoes on; her toes pointed upward, as if she didn't want them to touch the cork-tiled floor. From the back, my mother looked older than my grandmother, hunched over, her hair matted from lying in bed for so many days. When I heard their voices in the bedroom, I rubbed my forearm and saw there the imprint of my mother's fingers. The crooked oblongs were a deep, angry red, the red of an unripe plum.

With nothing behind her, my mother invested all of herself in her daughter. This is evident in one of the few home movies I've seen of the times when I was a baby. This one my grandmother gave me just before she died. In it, my grandfather frolics with me in a circle, tenderly hold-ing my tiny hand as if he were foxtrotting, smiling and obviously speaking or singing in a soft voice, though the film has no sound. Our eyes are locked in mutual affection.

Then my mother, who is here about thirty years old and has styled my hair just like hers, in a high ponytail and white bow, takes me in her arms and imitates my grandfather's dance. But for her, everything is in a foreign tongue, even the language of love and motherhood. She begins to twirl faster, as if her intensity would convey the depth of her love and the roller-coaster ride would bind me to her and her alone.

Uncontrollably, dizzyingly, she dips me in a fierce seasickening spin and then throws me over her shoulder almost with abandon. Just as I'm about to right myself, she whirls full-speed in the other direction. Without support for my back and neck, my head and arms flail. Finally, my mother stops the ride and I work myself upright again. Woozy and confused, I lean back in her hold, distancing myself from her. The camera settles on my face. I am clearly terrified, eyes wide and mouth agape in a round, scared face about to break into crying.

That film clip reflects all that is right and all that is wrong with her mothering. She wants to love, needs to be loved, but doesn't know how to be loving or lovable. Her need is urgent, ravenous, and unabating; she centers her life on me. Having lost her only model and reservoir of maternal love, she doesn't really know how to mother. She imitates what she sees, but her need is so intense that, even in what should be a small, happy moment in a day, she clutches and smothers. In that film clip, I am her possession; motherhood, for her, is a way to alleviate her intense alienation.

For my mother, I am an avenue to restoration, restitution, resurrection. I am a replacement for her lost family. I embody the dreams and hopes, the love and emotion, that should have come from others in the family who were killed in the war, especially her mother. I bring meaning to her life and theirs.

Sometimes I see my relationship with my mother in those small Russian Matrushka dolls that neatly fit inside each other. In my mother's life, a small Matrushka doll lost a larger doll—her mother—and, for years, she stood alone. With the birth of her daughter, there were two Matrushka dolls again, but their relative sizes were reversed—the daughter held and protected the mother. I became her mother because she needed one more than I did.

Still, I am the daughter, too, the great hope. I am supposed to be a genuine escapee—one who truly flees the past. Free of the pain and the guilt of surviving, I should be able to experience the happiness she could never fully enjoy. In her mind, she was entitled to so much and no more.

When I was ten and our family returned from an unusual, delightful weekend of downhill skiing, I saw the limitations of her happiness. When we got home, she locked herself in the bathroom and sobbed wildly from behind the door. "What's wrong?" my father asked as he knocked. "Didn't we have a good weekend?" She refused to open the door, but yelled from what seemed like the other side of a gulf. "Yes, we had a wonderful time. But I don't think I will ever have a day like this again. I have never been so happy and I doubt I'll ever be again. I don't deserve it."

So my mother directed herself toward me because I did deserve happiness. Through me, she hoped to experience a childhood, an adolescence, a parent-child relationship. She hoped to taste some of everyday life, experience normality, and, ultimately, even heal a part of herself. I became the past, the present, and the future.

But the past, which took a great toll on her, exacted a toll on me as well. This was never her intention. In her desperation to replace the mother love she had lost, she took from me more than I could give, more than she had a right to need. She lost her childhood to the war, and, in a way, I lost my childhood to her.

Knowing all this, I still find myself hoping, dreaming, praying—though I'm not a believer—that the baby I carry on this trip to Germany will be a daughter. I suppose I'm looking for my own repair, to give my daughter a childhood. So much of parenting is really self-parenting; it is a form of redemption. I know the dangers, yet I can't deny the instinct.

I want a daughter who isn't emotionally constricted by the war or even its aftermath. I want her to be raised in a place where the past and the present are not unhealthily intertwined, choking each other, as tight as a climbing vine that strangles a tree. I want her to escape the matrix of this family's maternal line.

I know that the war's legacy is formidable and infinite, but with each generation its life is divided in half. Maybe the effects in the next generation will be muted. Maybe my daughter can have what my grandmother, my mother, and even I couldn't have, what the mothers of the last two generations tried but failed to give their children: a life free of the war.

Chapter 6

Over breakfast, Mom scans the local German newspaper, the *Darmstadter Echo*, as I sip my second cup of tea and gaze at the large paper cup on the table. It's a miniature trash can, ready and waiting to swallow the debris of our meal—used plastic jelly containers, empty sugar packets, dirty napkins. What a simple, clean, efficient idea. Ahhhhh, those Germans, I think, feeling a twinge of awe at this smallest evidence of their knack for cleanliness and order.

"I can't believe this," Mom suddenly sputters from behind the page.

"What?" I say, startled out of my reverie about German ingenuity. As I look up, shafts of sunlight pour through the window next to the table, blinding me as I turn toward Mom and squint.

"There's a story in the paper about me coming back here," she says, dropping the newspaper to face me through the dust motes circling in the sunbeam.

"Really?" I'm amazed that the whole town already knows we're here. But, looking at Mom, I see that this article has brought a kind of ominous weather front, completely changing the landscape of her face.

"What does it say?" I ask.

"Wait, let me see," she mutters, brow furrowed above her glasses, teeth set.

"Boy, word gets around here fast," I grumble while trying to read German upside down. "Who could have told the newspaper already?"

"Maybe Hans. Or those men at the Town Hall."

"What does it say?" I ask again.

"Let's see if I can translate." She places the paper flat on the table, supports her forehead in her hands, carefully angles her head, and narrows her eyes to shield her view from the glaring sunlight reflecting off her half-glasses. In a tentative, broken cadence, like a child who has just learned to read, she begins:

"'Edith Schumer née Westerfeld left Germany during the Nazi regime and now has come back to Stockstadt, where she had lived for twelve years and attended school. The sixty-five-year-old was determined to come for a visit to break down the barriers.

"'Traveling with her daughter, she plans to see how the town has changed and find papers about what happened to her parents and their land.

"'After she left for America in 1938, she lived with an uncle until she finished her education as a nurse. She married and had two children. Today she lives in a suburb of Chicago and is a grandmother.

"'She and her daughter will be in Germany for one week.'"

"Where'd they get all that?" I ask. "I don't remember telling Hans those details. Did you give all that information to those men in the Town Hall?"

"I don't know," she says. "Maybe some reporter talked to Hans and the men and that's what they came up with.

"But I don't care that it's in the paper," she adds with irritation. "It's the headline that bothers me."

"What is it?"

"*Die Jüdin Edith Westerfeld besucht Stockstadt*," she reads, pointing to bold, black print and then she translates, "The Jew Edith Westerfeld visits Stockstadt."

"'The Jew'!" I am incredulous.

"Seeing that in print—'*Die Jüdin*'—makes me wonder why I came back here. Maybe nothing has changed," she says. "What was I thinking?"

"*Die Jüdin*" looks like a four-letter word, graffiti-scrawled in black paint. I'm overcome by an urge to white it out or rip it from the paper so that my mother doesn't have to look at it. I want to shield her from pain, as I do so often. This trip won't let me do that; I wonder what I was thinking.

"I don't like it either," I say weakly, lacking a better response. But then I think, wait a minute, try to consider the German point of view. "What should they have said?" I ask. "I mean, headlines have to be brief, and they often oversimplify or misstate things."

My mother looks unconvinced. "I suppose they could have used a few extra letters and written 'Jewish refugee Edith Westerfeld,'" I concede. "That doesn't sound so coarse."

Then again, everyone is identified by nationality in Europe, whose population holds far more purebreds than the American melting pot. Here, they call themselves the Frenchman, the Spaniard, the Croatian, whatever.

"Maybe that's the way they can identify you," I offer. "That's how they remember you, as Jewish."

"I suppose," she says, pondering the idea. "But it sounds like nothing has changed. 'The Jew.' It just gives me a bad feeling, a bad taste in my mouth."

"Me, too," I say. In fact, as I mull this, it makes me feel like spitting in disgust. Again, my mother and I are united in our otherness; the magnets pull us toward one another. The word "Jew" is so loaded and makes the Germans seem so obtuse.

Than a line in the article replays in my head. "Edith Schumer née Westerfeld left Germany. . . ." Left?

"And I like the euphemism on how you 'left Germany during the

Nazi regime.' Like you, a child of twelve, simply decided, It's time to be moving along," I say, smirking, then add, "Sounds like a bit of revisionist history to me."

"Yeah. And how about this line that I came to break down barriers?" she says, perturbed and pointing to the second sentence. "Why do I have to break down barriers? Did I put them up?

"I don't know about this," Mom finally says, her face in a scramble. Then she shakes her head in bewilderment. "I thought things would be different now." She stops, her face hangs with disappointment, and she says, "I thought I'd feel less left out. I thought I could come and make peace with the past. But . . ." She turns to me with pleading eyes. "But now I don't know if I can do this trip."

In a strange way, it was true. My mother had come to Germany seeking acceptance from those who had ostracized her. Her return would create a new, happier sense of the place whose previous memory had tormented her. The new would bury, whitewash, somehow muffle the old. Things would be different now. She would come and break down barriers, theirs and hers.

My mother spent years feeling that she was to blame for what had happened so many years ago. She took personally her banishment from Germany. Like a child who has been excluded on the playground by her classmates, she felt that the Germans had marked her as unwanted and unlovable.

She fought that characterization at every turn, demonstrating her self-worth through such selfless acts as becoming a nurse. Her compassion, her generosity, her empathy were extreme; everyone was her patient. She would do anything for almost anyone, never saying no to her family, a neighbor, even strangers.

Often as a child, I would become irritated with her because I sensed people could take advantage of her, asking her for favors they knew no one else would do. They could always count on her. Her need to be needed was so great that she even took dogs into her home when their owners went on vacation. Sometimes she would have five dogs in the house, each locked up in a different room. For this, she charged less than a boarding kennel.

When she had more dogs in the house than she could handle, she would get annoyed at herself. "I should never have taken this on," she'd say. But then she would excuse it: she just couldn't say no to the owner of that cocker spaniel.

Though I love dogs, my mother's small business puzzled and irritated me. Obviously, the money didn't justify the trouble. Why, I wondered, would anyone want the responsibility, the noise, the mess? "Mom," I would ask in exasperation, "what do you do this for?" She couldn't really give me an answer. But now I see that it was another act from which she derived a sense of value, another way to prove her worthiness to the world.

To heal completely, I think, she needed to show even the Germans that she is good. She came here in the same spirit that brings many people to a reunion—to show that she is not what they thought she was. She wants to reconcile; she wants to feel they don't hate her anymore because she is "*die Jüdin*."

Hans bounds into the restaurant, spry in a light-brown cap and old-fashioned jacket, again surprising me with the energy of this man in his sixties. He pulls up a chair and surveys the empty cups and dirty plates at our table.

"Good morning," he booms enthusiastically as he takes off his cap and sits down. "How are you today?"

"Okay," my mother mutters, coldly, barely acknowledging his arrival.

"Everything all right? How were the accommodations?" he asks, maybe suspecting that we were dissatisfied with the hotel, which he had assured us was good.

"Fine," I tell him. My mother still hasn't even looked at him.

Then he picks up the paper, which is folded to frame the story, and says, "Ahhh, I see you saw the article in today's paper." He smiles and then turns to Mom. "That's who called me away from our museum tour yesterday, the reporter from the paper."

"Did you read the article?" I asked pointedly.

"Yes, I read it." His eyes, bright and smiling, don't register any indication that the article might have offended us.

"Well, what did you think?" I ask.

"I'm so pleased they put it on the top of page two and gave it that much space in the paper," he says excitedly. "I really wanted the *Echo* to write something to acknowledge that you're here and to welcome you back to Stockstadt."

Dumbfounded, my mother and I exchange a knowing glance. "They acknowledged we're here, all right," I tell Hans sardonically, "but I'm not sure we feel all that welcome."

"What?" His eyebrows arch higher than usual. "Why not?" He picks up the paper, rereading the article for any possible offenses.

"Some of the language makes us feel uneasy," I volunteer. "We didn't like that they called my mother 'the Jew' in the headline and said that she left Germany, rather than fled."

"Oh, I see." The line between his eyebrows forms, a deep crevice I first noticed when we talked about Kristallnacht yesterday; it seems to deepen with worry. He rereads the article as more of his forehead sinks into the crevice.

Then he adds delicately, "They meant no harm."

"I thought we could . . . Ohhh, I don't know," Mom says, staring through the window at the view of several massive, deeply rooted oak trees that were saplings long before any of us were born. Clearly, she is not addressing Hans or me, but the stand of trees, maybe all of Germany. "I guess I thought things would be different. I thought I could come back here and take away the ache."

"It is different," Hans says, reassuringly touching my mother's arm. She pulls away slightly. "We were trying to welcome you back, make you feel special here. How can we identify you except as a Jew? That's how we remember you. They did not mean it, how do you say, to be insulting. You must give us a chance."

"I don't know," Mom says, still leaning away from his outstretched hand. "It makes me feel uncomfortable. Maybe we should go back home now."

"No, please, give us a chance," he says insistently, trying to get her to look at him directly. "I wouldn't have told the paper if I had known that the article would make you feel this way. Please," he begs, his words urgent and sincere, "I've planned so many things for the week. You can't go back now."

"But I doubt I can feel comfortable here," my mother says, biting her lip and looking like a child fleeing a bully, yearning to go home to comfort and security. Finally, she looks at him, but tucks her arm tightly against her body, avoiding his reach.

"You can't judge us all by one newspaper article. Please, you can't leave."

He waits for his words to penetrate. When he sees that she is unmoved, his eyes turn to me, asking if I can't do something. I look at him and gently shrug my shoulders, indicating that this is her decision.

"We're planning a reunion for you Wednesday," he blurts out in desperation. "I wanted it to be a surprise but must tell you now. The whole class from grammar school is going to get together for coffee and cake. You are to be the guest of honor."

"I don't know."

"Don't disappoint us," he appeals. "This is important to us. We need to do this for you." He reaches for her arm again and holds her firmly.

"I don't know," she murmurs, dodging his gaze.

"Your being here not only helps you to heal; it helps us, too. Please. Don't take that away from us . . . from any of us.

"Besides, you must stay," he says, completely changing the tone of his voice to a loud whisper. "I found out where Mina lives." He darts a quick glance behind him, as if he were afraid that someone would hear him say her name.

When she hears Mina's name, my mother's eyebrows rise with keen interest and she turns her whole body toward him. This is his trump card. She wouldn't want to leave Germany without seeing Mina, and Hans is the only person we know who can direct us to her.

"Oh, really? Where? Where is she now?" My mother fires questions as if she can't get the information fast enough.

"In a little village in the Odenwald Mountains called Tromm."

"Trawm?" My mother mispronounces it slightly. "How far is it?"

"Yes, Tromm. It's about an hour from here. It shouldn't be too hard to find, though it's not on the maps. It's very small, only a few houses in the town."

"Why would she live there?" my mother asks.

"When she and her husband left Stockstadt after the war, they moved to the mountains to run a kind of bed and breakfast where tuberculosis patients came to recover. Dozens of sick people would come to Mina's mountain retreat and stay for months, recovering and breathing the clean air. But now she's living there by herself, I think.

"Once we find the town," he adds, "it'll be easy to find her. Maybe we can arrange to go Friday."

With clasped hands, imploring clear blue eyes, Hans waits like a lawyer who has approached the bench. My mother weighs his case, turning toward the window again and sitting quietly, her eyes scanning the trees as if they were following a squirrel.

I suspect we will continue our trip. She wants to see Mina again. In addition, his need will melt her. She is a good person who can't say no and will hurt herself before she disappoints others.

"Well, then," she says, straightening herself. "Okay. I suppose we'll see how it goes."

"*Ah, danke. Danke.*" Hans lapses into German before my mother has gotten the last word out. "Thank you," he says to me, smiling with relief. "I'm so pleased." The crevice in his forehead immediately disappears into a shadowy line, and his body, wiry and stiff a moment ago, has lost its tension as he leans back in his chair.

Then my mother folds the paper, tucks it into the outside pocket of her large purse, and adds, "We can always decide to leave."

~

Hans insists that he cannot go anywhere until he visits his son's grave, as he does every day. He asks us to join him; we can't refuse. On our half-mile walk from the hotel to the cemetery located next to the train station, a woman, who appears to be around my mother's age, accosts us.

"*Edith*," she greets my mother excitedly, "*Edith. Kannst du dich noch an mich erinnern?* Remember me?" She takes my mother's limp hand and holds it as Hans translates for me, "*Kannst du dich noch erinnern? Natürlich, ich kenne dich noch.* Remember me? Of course you do."

My mother searches her countenance for some defining feature that age has not eroded. Nothing registers, and she stares at the woman blankly.

"*Ich bin Emma Landauer.*" But, obviously, her name doesn't offer much of a clue.

"*Ahhhhh, ja, ja,*" my mother says, and begins to act less foggy, though I'm quite sure she doesn't remember this woman. The three of them talk in German for a few minutes, and then I pick up in their goodbyes that they will see each other Wednesday. So my mother let on that the reunion is no longer a surprise.

"I don't remember her at all," my mother says to Hans. "I'll never remember all their names on Wednesday. They'll all know me and I'm not going to know any of them."

"It'll come back to you," Hans says. "You'll remember, and I'll help you out."

"Funny," Mom adds, as we continue our walk, "she said when one classmate called about the reunion, he asked her to guess who would be the surprise guest. She said she knew immediately it would be me. 'Figuring it out wasn't hard,' Emma said, 'since no other classmate has left Stockstadt.'"

The cemetery looks like a rock garden; stones and burial sites are tightly crammed next to each other, with almost no room for grass. Family members who come each day to bring fresh flowers meticulously maintain the graves and clean the stones, Hans explains. "*Guten Tag*"—he waves in greeting to several people. Maybe he sees them here every day. They seem to care for the grave sites as if they were visiting a loved one in a hospital.

"Why are there so many stones in such a small space?" I whisper.

"Land is expensive and we have little space for cemeteries," Hans explains. "The state digs up graves after thirty years unless the family buys the land. But few can afford it. The land costs nearly thirty thousand dollars. If a family doesn't buy the land, new graves are placed on top of the old. So many graves from the families are gone now."

"So do you rent the plot from the state?" I ask.

"Yes," he says. "That's right."

"What about the Jewish cemeteries?" I ask. "Are they dug up now, since more than thirty years have passed?"

"I . . . I don't know," he says, and then, after thinking about it, he elaborates. "I don't think so. This is a fairly recent policy, affecting newer graves. But we'll have to see.

"You know," he adds after a few minutes, "I've never been to the Jewish cemetery. I don't even know where it is."

I am struck by this policy on graves. Intentionally or not, it serves to restrict what's known about the past. How convenient for the Germans to legislate this tidy way, seemingly dictated by simple necessity, of cutting off any remembrance extending back more than thirty years. Memory is made just long enough for one generation to keep the previous generation alive; it reveals only one link in a long chain.

We stand before the grave of Hans's son. Hans places flowers on the stone and fusses with them. Then he stands next to my mother, who has been watching him closely.

"It is so hard to live without him," Hans tells her. "I know something of what you've lived through."

He does not say how his son died. The marker's simple, moving epitaph makes me wonder who he was and what happened to him.

GUENTHER HERMANN
1959–1989
I am where you are. I am who you think I am.

I think of my mother's mother. I have always felt an urgent need to invent a relationship, a life where there is none. The living take a part of the dead with them, carrying them around in their minds, like a song that lingers after the music has been turned off. Though I never laid eyes on my grandmother, never heard her voice, I still can hear her faint song.

Since I cannot know her, I have collected details to construct my grandmother and make her real. A few years ago, I asked my mother how tall she was. "It was fifty years ago when I last saw her," she said, as if it was to be expected that she shouldn't remember those details. "I was only twelve, not full-grown myself."

Still, I persisted. "Was she a lot taller than you then?"

"I don't remember," she replied, uttering the sentence that to this day decisively ends any conversation she doesn't want to pursue.

But I need to know. I didn't want my grandmother to become a blur in the receding past. So I would use details to keep her in view, to give her a life in my imagination, hoping that, if I accumulated enough information, I might somehow assemble her like a toy and—who knows—restore her magically to life.

"Can you tell me anything about Frieda Westerfeld?" I ask Hans, trolling for a piece to add to the collage that is my grandmother.

"What is it you want to know?" he asks.

"Well, anything really," I say. "Tell me what she was like."

"She was . . ." He pauses and then starts again. "I saw her when . . ." He stops himself; several seconds pass, and I realize he's not going to finish his sentence.

I try to pick up the thread of his thought. "When was the last time you saw my grandmother?" I ask. "What was she wearing?"

Hans has turned away from me so that I can't see his face. When he looks at me again, he snaps. "I know what you want to know, but it is

very delicate." His eyes are rimmed with tears; these events, these feelings, half a century old, lurk so close to his emotional surface. The image of the bullet-ridden skull from the museum flashes in my mind.

"I will tell you the truth when I'm ready," he says, then he walks over
to his son's grave, picks up a broom, and vigorously sweeps the gravestone, stirring up gray clouds of dirt.

Chapter 7

"When I came this way this morning," Hans says, as we walk through the cemetery gate to begin our tour of the town of Stockstadt, "I saw Klara Franz. You remember her, don't you?"

"Klara Franz? I'm not sure," Mom repeats, puzzling over the name and running through her mental Rolodex all the people she ever knew in Germany. "Franz, Franz."

"She was your sister's best friend. Remember? The two were inseparable."

"Ohhhh, yes," Mom replies, "I can sort of picture her—a short, cute girl with reddish-blond hair and freckles."

"Well, yes." Hans breaks into a slow, wide grin. "Fifty years ago.

"I remember the two would walk past my house every day on their way to school," he continues. "They would giggle and tell secrets. A few times, I tried to walk with them, but I always felt like they didn't want me there."

"Yes," she says, "now I remember. I felt the same way when they would play at our house. They always had their private games. They would spend hours coming up with their own rules so that no one else could play with them."

"I think Klara is still outside working in her garden," Hans says, shifting on his toes to look off in the distance. "Yes, there she is. She's the woman in the front yard several houses down. She's wearing dark clothes with a scarf on her head." He points to a figure in the distance. "Let's go say hello."

I see a round woman hunched over the last of the faded yellow mums in her little garden. She wears a long, full skirt and a brown sweater, her frizzy, gray-blond hair straying in spikes from the scarf tied behind her neck. One hand clutches dead plants, roots, and leaves; the other holds a small spade that she jabs, over and over, into the hard soil with a vigorous wrist action. Intent on her work, she never glances up; I can't see her face yet.

"*Guten Tag*," Hans calls to her to get her attention.

"*Guten Tag*," she mutters, a generic hello tossed at whoever is passing.

"Klara," Hans tries again. "Excuse me, Klara, I'd like you to meet someone," he says in German. "This is Edith. Edith Westerfeld." For once, I know what he's saying, if only because it's right out of Lesson One on the German audiotape course I mastered just before the trip.

"*Guten Tag*," she repeats, her eyes still fixed on her mums. One side of her face, slightly freckled and the only part I've seen, reddens as she weeds. Her round hands, surprisingly large for a woman's, are sheathed in an uneven glove of dirt. Dark crescent moons tip each finger.

"Klara," Hans starts again. He says something with the word "*Schwester*" and then my aunt's name. He must be reminding her that Betty Westerfeld is my mother's sister, her childhood friend.

Finally, she stops digging, casts a blank look at Hans, and says weakly, "*Wen?*" I assume that means "What?" or "Who?" Her steely gray eyes look uninterested, if not downright suspicious; clearly she doesn't want to be bothered.

"*Betty Westerfeld*," Hans says again, emphasizing the German "V." Then he says something I don't understand and points down the road. I assume he's trying to prompt her memory, indicating where Mom's family lived or where she and my aunt played.

"*Westerfeld? Nein*," she says as if she were talking to someone who had called on the phone and dialed the wrong number. She shakes her head, then returns to her square of dirt and sticks her spade into soil she already weeded. She hasn't even looked at Mom.

Hans shifts his boots on specks of gravel strewn on the sidewalk. He rubs one foot back and forth, like a bull about to charge. Gravel flies from under his foot. Mom watches the woman weed almost without blinking.

"Let's go." I turn to Hans, breaking the prolonged silence.

"Yes," he agrees, before I've gotten out the "o" in "go." "Let's go."

He leads us away without the customary "*Auf Wiedersehen*." A few steps later, I look back, narrowing my eyes at Klara Franz. She catches my glance, veers away at once, and returns to weeding with her broad, rough hands.

We walk about a half-mile; then, around the corner from the Town Hall, Hans takes us into a small store that sells wine, newspapers, and magazines.

"Why are we here?" I ask, browsing at the postcards on a rack next to the cash register. Maybe he thought we'd like to pick up a few. I pull out one that pictures a typical Tudor German house, then put it back. My husband might like it, but my sons would rather get something that speaks to them: a picture of a knight, a war monument showing soldiers, or the ruins of a medieval castle.

As I weigh which card to buy, the lump in my throat rises and begins to choke me. Subtracting six hours from my watch, I figure that it's 5:00 A.M. in Chicago. My sons are asleep. I picture the hundreds of times I've sat at their bedside taking in their calm, loosely muscled faces as they dreamed, eyes fluttering and rolling behind the screens of their eyelids, their tiny sausage fingers jerking and twitching with life.

How I wish I could see them now and know for sure that they're sound asleep. If they are, they're unaware of my absence. For now, at least, they're not yearning for me as I am for them. Not until they wake up in about an hour and call, "Mom. Mo-o-o-o-mmmm?"

I scan the other postcards—pictures of the Rhein, a green-and-yellow vineyard on a steep hill, a quaint church. Finally, I settle on one from a nearby museum that exhibits old weapons, figuring that all of them will like it.

"Do you know where we are?" Hans asks my mother.

She looks around the shop, suddenly confused and lost. "No," she replies. "Where are we?"

"Look outside." The peculiar look on Hans's face persuades me to put the postcard on the counter and walk back through the entrance to look around with my mother. The building we were in sits twenty feet back from the road and has a large swath of pavement, as wide as a driveway, in front of it. The rest of the buildings are situated closer to the curb.

Across the street, I notice a satellite dish next to the Town Hall. A couple of shops down, at the video store, a poster in its window of J.R., Miss Ellie, and Sue Ellen announces newly available tapes of the TV series *Dallas*.

"Ohhh my," my mother says frantically, rushing past me and back through the door to Hans. I'm right behind her as she grabs Hans's arm to look directly into his eyes.

"Is this my house?" she asks imploringly.

"Yes," he says. A slight smile edges his lips. "This is it."

"I knew it," she says breathlessly, as she brushes hair off her face with a trembling hand. "I recognized it by the space in front of the building. The children in the area would come to play games in front of our house."

"I thought you'd remember that," he says. "Even I played here a few times."

"But what happened to the house?" Mom asks, her eyes searching the shop.

"They have rebuilt most of it, but I think there are a few parts that weren't touched. We'll find the shop owner, who also lives in the house behind the shop, and ask if we can go inside."

The owner, Günter Frey, turns out to be a tall man of about forty, with a shock of black, frizzy hair in which a few coarse gray strands insist on separating from the rest. When he comes out from his house to meet my mother, his face appears tense and businesslike. Without a smile, he barely says hello. Instead, he launches into a defensive diatribe that Hans translates for me, talking fast to keep up with Frey's German.

"I got the house from my father," he explains nervously, as if he knew this day would come and he had prepared a speech for it. "I did not buy it myself; I inherited it. My father bought the house from . . . from your father."

My mother tries to interrupt him, I suspect to clarify that we have not come to reclaim the house. But he won't let her say a word.

"It is important that you understand that I have owned this house only since 1970. It was falling apart then, so we had to tear most of it down and rebuild it. Before that time, my father's name was on the deed."

"*Bitte schön*," she interrupts him. "Please, please," Hans continues to translate. "We just wanted to look around."

As she finishes her sentence, Hans whispers to me, "Frey doesn't want us to think that he had any dealings or anything to do with the Nazis." Maybe not, but I don't believe his father was so innocent.

"Ahhh," Frey says now, his face relaxing so that his good looks are more apparent. "That would be fine. Let me show you what we have done."

Inside, Frey explains that most of the house has been redesigned, but some original wood was used to trim the new rooms. We walk through a long hallway that opens into a living room. My mother stops, looks around, purses her lips. Then her eyes shine as she breaks into a pleasant smile.

"This looks a little like the original house," she says. "We had a long hallway here where my father had installed the first telephone in town. All the neighbors would come to our house to borrow the phone. Someone was always standing here in the hallway, leaning into the receiver, and yelling at the top of his lungs."

She is drawn toward a back window in the living room that overlooks the garden and large yard. Staring out, she says, "This looks just the same. Each fall, my father would build a *succah* right there." She points to a large space, clear of trees. "It was my favorite time of year—so colorful." She dreamily gazes out and then asks me with a significant look, "Do you know what a *succah* symbolizes?"

"No, what?" Here and now, she's giving me a lesson in Jewish history?

"It's like a little hut," she explains. "It's a symbol for the homes the Israelites used when they wandered the desert for forty years, when they had no permanent home." I mull over her answer for a moment, and then I wonder if she is trying to tell me that this house wasn't a permanent home either.

Frey calls us over and proudly points to an old wooden beam in the living-room ceiling that has some Hebrew engraving on it. "This is from the original house," he says. "It was a structural support inside the wall. I doubt you've seen it before."

My mother looks up and says, "No, I don't think so." Then she shuffles her feet, twists her body, cranes her neck, and shifts her head from side to side. She takes a step, turns around, and contorts her body in another position.

"What are you doing?" Frey asks.

"It's upside down," my mother tells him in German as Hans continues to translate for me. "The beam. It's upside down."

"Upside down?" says Frey, clearly disturbed. "What do you mean? How can this be?"

"You put in the beam upside down and backward."

"But we consulted a rabbi," he says.

"Well, what did he tell you?"

"He told us what it says, but I didn't think to ask which way it reads."

"Well, the way you have it, it reads from left to right," my mother says emphatically. "Hebrew reads from right to left."

Frey shakes his head, drops his gaze to the floor like a child who has just been reprimanded, and mutters something.

"Oh," Hans says, "I don't know how you translate what Frey says. He's disappointed and disgusted to learn that the beam is backward. He

says—how do you say in English—uh, 'for goodness' sake.'" After a moment, Frey says something else to my mother and Hans translates, "I'm
sorry."

That seems to me to be a displaced apology. Of all things, Frey feels
he has insulted my mother by installing the beam improperly?

"What does the beam say, Mom?" I ask. I wouldn't have known the
beam was upside down either, since I received no religious training and
cannot read a word of Hebrew. But my mother was raised in a religious
household. She once mentioned that her parents insisted she go to Hebrew school even in the middle of winter, when her toes would freeze
on the ten-kilometer bike ride to the rabbi's house in the next town.

After the war, however, she had little use for religion. When I asked
her why, she said, "I want nothing to do with it. Look what happened in
Germany—that was among mostly Christian people. After that, I
couldn't trust any religion. I just couldn't believe in God. Besides, without my family, I didn't want to go to temple anymore."

Still, she never renounced Judaism. Though she didn't go to temple
on the High Holidays, she didn't go to work either. When I asked why,
if she didn't believe, she stayed home, she would say, "I am Jewish. What
else can I be?"

Though my mother probably hasn't looked at a Hebrew sentence
since she left Germany, she seems to remember the language. "It says a
Hebrew blessing on the house. It has our family name, Westerfeld, on it,
and the year our family built the house, 1721."

As I study the deep, arcane carvings in the old timber and muse on
the new, backward setting of the beam, something I read not long ago
pops into my head: "We can be very cruel," said poet Liesl Mueller.
"Later we sentimentalize the people we have injured."

Frey leads us down a back staircase toward a dank, dark space that's
clearly older than the rest of the house. "I think you will remember
this," he says, ducking to avoid hitting his head on the low ceiling above
the staircase. Hans translates as we descend upon uneven, unsteady
wooden steps.

At the bottom, my mother looks around the space, built of old stone,
patched with concrete, paved in dirt. Rafters run along the ceiling,

joined neatly at tongue-in-grooves, like puzzle pieces. This construc-
tion, which Hans says was first used to build old ships, doesn't require
nails. It is the original foundation.

"We stored apples and potatoes on shelves here in the basement for
the winter," my mother says, pointing to a foundation wall. "It was our
refrigerator. In the fall, we would line up hundreds of apples and potatoes like marching bands. They couldn't touch each other or else they
would spoil. I was in charge of spacing them."

Then she points to an old shelf of splintered wood hanging from the
stone wall near the cellar's low ceiling. Several pieces of heavy pottery
are placed haphazardly on the shelf. About a dozen gray-and-beige
sealed crocks remain; all are discolored and dirty with age, and a couple
are deeply cracked, but they are not falling apart.

"I don't think anyone's touched that shelf since I left," she marvels.
"That's exactly how I remember it. The big one was always on the end."
She points to the largest container. "We kept our preserves in those
crocks. We stored pickles, onions, corn, and fruits." It's possible that the
crocks still contain their original contents. "We would jar everything,"
she says. Suddenly, a cat appears, rubs up against my mother's leg as she
finishes her thought. "That way, we had those things to eat all winter."

Looking at the cat tenderly, she squats down to pet it. "Ye-e-e-ss," she
coos, "you're sweet." As she scratches its throat, it supplely twists
through her hands and feet, its tail curling near her face and its purr mo-
toring loudly. "She looks just like the two we had when I was a child,"
Mom says, and her eyes brighten.

My mother mentioned her cats to me once, when I lived in a house
with a mouse problem. She had suggested we get a cat, like the ones her
family had in Germany. They kept them to kill mice, she explained, but
to her they were pets; she would sneak food from her dinner plate and
feed them. I suppose she worried about what happened to those cats after she left.

"She has the same white paws and calico head," my mother says, running her hand along the ridge of its back to the end of its tail. "And the
same white-tipped tail." Maybe, I think, this cat is a descendant of my
mother's pet.

She stands, looks at the shelf again, throws her head back, closes her eyes dreamily, and draws a deep breath through her nose. "The smell is just the same." Smells, I think, may be the last thing on earth to die. In an enclosed, dark cellar, an odor could linger forever. Here, a heavy, moldy smell of standing water persists; I close my lips tightly to quell my nausea. But my mother drinks it in. The familiar aroma is its own embrace, welcoming her home.

"It's strange," my mother says to me, unaware of my discomfort, maybe even of me. "It's just how I remembered it." Her wide eyes soak up the surroundings. The cat mews in a corner of the basement; its greenish eyes pierce the dimness, luminescent as the face of a glow-in-the-dark clock.

"It feels the same," she continues, "yet so little of my house remains."

"Still," she says, walking toward the old steps, "I feel like I'm home again. I can feel myself as a little girl coming in after playing in the garden."

Frey, Hans, and I watch her intently. Swept up by memory and pulled into its back roads, she walks over to the wall under the shelf and rubs her hand back and forth along the bumpy stones. Then she stops, leans over, and picks up a fistful of the dirt floor. Slowly she rocks her hand, sieving fine gray dirt through her fingers like sand in an hourglass. When her hand is empty, she keeps it cupped and outstretched, but stands perfectly still and cocks her head slightly, to listen for something or someone.

"What do you hear?" I ask. She narrows her eyes, listens more intently, turns, and slowly takes several steps toward the staircase.

"I can almost hear my mother calling me."

My mother wants to visit the Jewish cemetery in the next town where her family had burial plots. So we return to the hotel to get the car from the parking lot. Before leaving, my mother goes up to the room to get her jacket while Hans and I wait near the front desk.

"*Fräulein Westerfeld, er uh, Frau Schumer,*" the man behind the desk calls to her as she joins us, "*Frau Schumer.*"

"Yes," she answers. He hands her a fistful of phone messages. "What's this?" she asks me rather than him. She reads the pink notes, each with a different German name and phone number on it. "They must be my classmates. I sort of remember some names." About five called, leaving messages that they were looking forward to the reunion or just to say, "*Hallo* and *Willkommen*."

Hans gets in the back so my mother can sit in the passenger seat and I steer the red Rabbit down a side street about half a block from the hotel. Suddenly a woman dressed in street clothes and house slippers comes running out of her front door toward us, yelling, "*Edith, Edith!*"

Catching up with the car, she raps on my window. "*Anhalten, anhalten,*" she says to me. I stop the car and lower the window and she pokes her head in, speaking around me in German. My mother exchanges a few words with her, but Hans doesn't translate.

After a few minutes, they say goodbye. "How did she know it was you?" I ask immediately. "She couldn't possibly have recognized you after all these years."

"No, she didn't," Hans says. "She said she saw that the car was rented by its oval plates. Very few people in town drive rented cars. So she figured it was your mother."

"I feel like . . . like a celebrity," Mom says, a little dazed from the attention. "I didn't expect all this."

Hans doesn't know exactly where the Jewish cemetery is located in the town, so we have to ask strangers for directions. My mother says, "Let's see if I can make myself understood," as she rolls down her window and calls to a man in a dark suit, a businessman walking leisurely down the street.

"*Wo ist der jüdische Friedhof?*" she calls to him. Where is the Jewish cemetery?

Startled, the man slows slightly, then quickly picks up his pace, brushes his hand in the air, and mumbles something without looking at her.

"What did he say?" I ask, as she closes the window.

"It's great he understands my German," she says. "But did you see? He didn't even look at me. He said he couldn't tell me where it is. He didn't know."

She looks around, spots another candidate, and says, "I'll ask him." I pull up so she can speak to an older man dressed in dirty work clothes—camouflage jacket, work boots, and a cap.

"*Wo ist der jüdische Friedhof?*" she inquires as she rolls down the window. He gives her a brief, one-sentence response and then continues on his way.

"What did he say?" I ask, as I make the car crawl along the side of the road.

"He said, 'You shouldn't go there.'"

"Why not?" I ask.

"He didn't tell me," she says. "It's strange. Nobody looks me in the eye when I talk to them. They all cringe when I say the word *Jüdische*, like it's a dirty word. They all squirm."

"I suppose," Hans volunteers, after quietly watching this scene from the back seat, "people don't know where it is."

"So how do we find it?" I ask.

"Let's go to one of the other cemeteries," Hans says, "and ask if the caretaker knows where it is."

Hans directs us to the public cemetery in the center of town. Here we find the caretaker, a man in his sixties dressed stylishly in jeans and a leather jacket, who speaks only German. But when he learns that we are from America, he proudly shows us the Levi's tag on his jeans and explains in broken English that his daughter lives in New York and sends them to him.

"*Wo ist der jüdische Friedhof?*" my mother asks.

Obviously puzzled and surprised, the man knits his eyebrows together. Clearly, no one has asked him that lately—maybe not ever. His eyes fix on my mother's face and he says, "*Wie?*," asking her to repeat herself.

"*Wo . . . Wo ist der jüdische Friedhof?*" she says. I watch his reaction closely. He isn't cringing or squirming, but seems shaken.

"It's here," Hans says, translating the man's German. "Who are you looking for?" he adds.

"Kahn," my mother answers.

"Kahn. Kahn," he incants. "Kahn.

"My father worked for the Kahn business," he says through Hans. "It was a leather business, right?"

"Yes," my mother says, "and they had a grocery store, too."

"How are you related to Kahn?"

"He was my grandfather," Mom says, saying "grandfather" with some pride, "*mein Grossvater*."

"Well, then," he says, "it's good that you've come." He points out the window at the graves in the distance.

"The cemetery is in the northeast corner of the public cemetery," he adds. "Go to my wife at our house, just up the street. She keeps a record of the Jewish graves. She can tell you where to find the ones you're looking for."

The modest brick house, just around the corner, is dark and the curtains are drawn; it looks as if no one is home. Mom hammers the door knocker, a once-handsome brass piece that has aged into a discolored brown.

We wait, but no one answers. Just when we are about to turn around and head back to the cemetery, a woman cracks open the door and the smell of soup cooking wafts through the thin crevice. "*Ja?*"

Hans tells her something in German. She opens the door and steps out onto the stoop. She's wearing old clothes and a scarf tied behind her neck. As Hans talks, she turns to look at Mom, then motions that she will be right back. In a minute she returns, and steps out onto the stoop waving a packet of fresh, typed pages.

"Who are you looking for?" she asks through Hans, leafing through the stapled pages—a list, I guess, of those families buried in the cemetery.

"My . . . my mother," she tells Hans. "Or my grandmother. Any of the Kahns."

As Hans translates my mother's answer, the woman repeats the name "Kahn." Then she locks her deep, doelike eyes on Mom; they glaze over and her lip trembles. The line between her eyebrows deepens as she fights tears, but they overpower her. She surrenders, pulling a tissue out of her pocket and openly dotting at her eyes.

"You, you know," she says, swallowing hard several times and licking her lips to dam her tears. "I . . . I knew your family." She is speaking very slowly and Hans takes long pauses between translated sentences. "I poured milk into jugs and delivered them in Worfelden where the Kahns lived. They were on my milk route.

"I am Jewish, but my husband is not," she says. She collects herself somewhat and continues. "My husband's family hid our family during the war. After it was all over, we were married. We always say Hitler was our matchmaker." A slight smile peeks out, like a brief appearance of the sun on a rainy day.

She stops talking as Hans catches up to her and then she continues. "Most of the Jews who stayed in Germany are married to non-Jews."

"Can I ask you," I say to Hans as if I were asking him, "what was it like to live as a Jew in Germany after the war?"

"It hasn't been easy," she says, more collected now, as if this subject is safer for her. "Even now, I'm not always comfortable, especially with the way many Germans have reacted to the past. It's strange. The people our age have hardly looked at themselves. They don't talk about it. They act as if they didn't know anything about it."

"*Wir haben nichts gewusst*," Hans repeats her German and then adds, " 'We knew nothing about this,' they say. 'We just didn't know.' "

"But how is it for you?" I ask again.

"For me," she says, "being here has not been easy. But I wouldn't have done it any other way."

"Did you ever think of leaving?" I ask.

"Yes, many times. But I just couldn't. I felt I had a duty to stay so that the Jews would go on here.

"Besides, where would I go? Germany is my home. Spending my life as a German was important to me." She pauses.

Then she adds, as if I needed to be reminded, "I am German."

~

"I'm not sure anything is back here," I tell Hans, as we walk through the manicured public cemetery toward the northeast corner. Here alone, the area looks like an overgrown field, neglected for decades.

"He said the northeast corner," Hans says. "This must be it."

A curtain of dead cattails, dried goldenrod, and brown grasses nearly as tall as I am shrouds the cemetery. The corner's ugly, unkempt state contrasts dramatically with the rest of the cemetery, like a housing project in the middle of an upscale neighborhood.

"The caretaker should have handed out a machete so we can get through," I remark.

Hans leads the way, hacking at the foliage with his arms, and then takes several steps; Mom and I follow in his path of mashed weeds, dodging plants that spring back into our faces. He stumbles, calls to us to "mind your feet," and then says, "I think I found something."

He flattens and clears some plants with his boots, unveiling a very old stone, discolored brownish-yellow in spots, that no longer stands upright. Vandals may have pushed it over, or it may have just toppled with time. The face of the stone is up, but its inscription, blurred by weather and age, is nearly impossible to read. I can make out a one and an eight in the year of birth—sometime in the 1800s.

A few feet ahead, Hans finds several standing gravestones. "Come here," he calls to us, clearing the cloak of tangled vines that have grown over the stones. Many are impossible to read, their lettering eroded by thousands of days of rain and snow. Now the wind rustles and whistles through these spindly weeds, providing eerie background to Mom's narrative of whatever she can decipher on the stones.

"Eighteen sixty-four to 1902," she says.

"Eighteen seventy-eight to 19-something."

"'*Geliebte Mutter*' means 'Beloved Mother' of someone. . . . Can you read the name?" she asks me, pointing to markings that look like not just a foreign language but some yet-undeciphered alphabet.

I squint, my eyes teary from the strain. The stone is clouded with gray, like the sediment in the bottom of a glass of tap water. "No, I can't read that one either."

Still, the stones eerily teem with death . . . and life . . . and stories.

Whole lives are noted in a few words—brief summaries edited further by nature. One marks the death of a newborn, only five months old; here is a young man, only twenty years old; here, an eighty-year-old grandmother.

But no one comes here. No one wants to hear these stories. Those who do, the descendants of the buried, no longer live in Germany; they can't care for the graves.

The Germans—the Germans wouldn't think of it. "You shouldn't go there," the man said, I suppose because they don't want to remember, don't want to know that this place exists. *Wir haben nichts gewusst*—we just didn't know . . . just don't want to know.

To the descendants of these dead, graves are all they can know. They're all that's left of their world. But it's difficult even to find the cemetery, let alone the graves of relatives. Seems to me, I think angrily, that if the government wants to offer Jews restitution we'll need more than government-issued airfare to come back and visit. We need maps to the Jewish cemeteries, where the government should catalogue and maintain the graves. At least a marker could be placed at each grave site, so that a visitor can identify who is buried there.

Meanwhile, my mother finds another cluster of graves. "Here are the Kahns," she calls to me. "Lisette Kahn. I don't remember her. I'm sure she's related to us. I just don't know how.

"Sol Westerfeld. He may have been my cousin's grandfather. I'm not sure."

Here, at last, is one she recognizes. "Max Kahn," she says, "oh, Max Kahn."

"Who is he?" I ask.

She presses her eyes shut and crinkles her eyelids, fighting for composure, staving off the emotional storm that is brewing within her. For so long, she has kept a lid on her feelings, mostly by deadening herself. But the name on this gravestone has shaken her, knocked her off her false equilibrium. When she opens her eyes, her face is bathed in tears.

"Max Kahn," she says, her voice altered by the heaviness in her throat, "was my grandfather.

"He was, he was my mother's father."

Her silence is broken as she publicly weeps for those she has privately, unceasingly mourned. I want to say something, maybe "I'm sorry," but that seems meaningless. I feel nothing but distance and numbness. I've never heard of this man; I know nothing of her life with him. My lack of feeling gives way to guilt: At this moment, I can't share her suffering, I can't know what has defined her. I am a generation once removed.

I touch her elbow gently, offering steady support. But she recoils. Instead, I stand close to her, so that our sweaters occasionally graze.

Hans, an unwitting and unwilling intruder on this extremely personal moment, busies himself with clearing other nearby graves. Or maybe I'm giving him more credit than I should; maybe he's oblivious to my mother's grief. I'm not sure.

I wait and wait for my mother to say something. I want to let her come back to the present when she's ready. But again, as I did during our flight here, I feel as if she's deep-sea diving while I wait anxiously at the surface. She stands perfectly still, tears streaming, for several long, edgy minutes.

At last, "I never expected to find a grave for him." I'm relieved to hear her voice. "I didn't know there was a grave for him. I wasn't sure when he died, but now I know." She adds in a whisper, "It was 1938."

"What do you remember about him?" I ask, hoping to glean whatever she's privately recalling.

"I remember my sister and I used to play dress-up in his furniture shop." She speaks slowly, working around the rock in her throat. "We would wrap ourselves in the fabrics he used for upholstering. Then we'd parade around the shop and he would laugh at our getup."

She stares quietly at the grave for a moment. "Seeing this reminds me of something he once said," she says. "We were visiting my grandparents for the New Year. It must have been 1935 and I was ten years old. The grown-ups were talking in his shop, and it was around the time Hitler had come to power. My grandfather kept joking and repeating a saying: 'Der Führer kommt weg, der Fünfer kommt an.'"

"What does that mean?" I ask when I realize she's not going to translate it.

"It means, 'The year '34 is going away, but the '5 is coming.' 'Four' in a different spelling in German meant *Führer*. So it meant that the Führer Hitler would be going away." She slowly lifts her hand, which looks gnarled and knobby against the gray stone. Tenderly, she runs a bent finger along the etched date on her grandfather's headstone: "He was so wrong."

She turns away. Her eyes scan the ground; then she picks up a pebble and places it on the ledge of the gravestone. It's one of the few Jewish customs I know, a signifier that a visitor has come and paid respect, that someone cared enough to remember the buried and the past.

Now Hans, who, I notice, has kept one eye on my mother, walks off, stomping plants with his boots and tussling with the overgrowth. I look at the surrounding graves, hoping that we might find my grandmother—though I know it is unlikely she is buried here or, for that matter, anywhere. I suppose she is an unknown soldier in an unmarked grave, along with most of the numbered others.

Hans returns to my mother's side. Still standing by my great-grandfather's grave, she allows her head to hang upon her chest sorrowfully, one hand clasping the other before her.

The wind cuts through the grasses in a high pitch as Hans fingers something in his hand. He leans over to place a small pebble next to my mother's on the gravestone.

Chapter 8

On our way to the reunion, we park the car in a lot next to the Rhein, the river my mother says she knew "intimately" as a child. As we climb out, she tosses Hans and me our sneakers from the back of the car. "You'll need these so that you can climb a little," she announces, trading her low heels for sneakers and rushing toward the water.

"Follow me," she says, with the confidence of a child who knows something no one else knows: what's here, she believes, is exactly as it was when she left. "I'll show you my favorite spot." She cuts through some bushes to a path that leads to a clearing. She walks along the edge of the water and then finds a flat rock.

"It's still here!" she says with delight. "This is it. I spent so many days here. I'd sit and watch the light and the water change colors." My mother and I stand on the rock and watch the light dance on the surface of the rich blue-green river, creating the illusion of stars sparkling. "It smells just the same," she says, happily inhaling a deep breath.

"Strange," she ponders, looking at the other side of the river. "It seemed so wide back then . . . so big. Now it seems like a little canal."

I recall the day, not long ago, when I peered through the windows of my elementary school and had that same odd perception. The desks in which I sat, the desks from which my feet couldn't touch the floor, now seemed dwarfed, as if they had shrunk since the last time I saw them.

As we head back to the car, I watch my mother stare at a woman passing us. Noticing my mother's gaze, the woman casually calls, "*Guten Tag.*"

"Why do you stare at her like that?" I ask.

"I don't know," she says. "It's funny. When I look at a face here, I expect to know who it is . . . even fifty years later. In Stockstadt, we knew everyone; every face had meaning." She thinks on that. "I suppose that's what it means to live in a small town."

"I have something for you back at the car," Hans says, "that will remind you of how small Stockstadt was when you were here." When he gets in the back seat, he reaches for his briefcase and pulls out some yellowed papers from a plastic case. The top sheet looks like some old official record, its formal words hand-lettered in an old-fashioned calligraphy.

"Look here," he says, showing us the crumbling, dog-eared page whose edges have browned like the Declaration of Independence. "It's the title transferring a piece of land to your family." He points to the signature of Isaak Westerfeld and the date—June 10, 1850.

Then he slowly pulls out another sepia-colored page. "This is the town's tax record from the year 1919. It shows who owned which properties in the area," he says, delicately turning the paper to let us read it. In the right corner, a blotch of black ink spilled a long time ago. The page lists fifty signatures, all with strikingly similar letter formations, all in the same slant. Hans points halfway down the page, to lines 324, 325, and 326. Scratched three times in black ink now faded to gray is a signature whose steady hand is barely contained in the designated lines: "Siegmund Westerfeld." My grandfather.

Instinctively, I gently rub the lines of the smooth paper, trying to finger the bumps of his name; I want to touch something he has touched.

I wonder, if I had known him, what name I would have called him.

~

The reunion is being held at a restaurant surrounded by a nature center. Hans wants us to see the animals that live here, so we arrive about twenty minutes early and find the room where the event will take place. Picture windows line the back wall, overlooking a large pond. The three of us watch small beige long-haired goats graze and cranes, geese, ducks, and swans, all with clipped, unbalanced wings, strut around the conservatory.

"That's quite a collection of exotic birds," I tell Mom as I survey the setting.

"Uh-huh," she says. An awkward-looking gray crane spreads its wings, attempts to swoop into the water for a fish, stumbles, and causes a huge splash. Water droplets hit the window.

"See any storks?" I ask Mom.

"No," she says, skeptically. She looks at me quizzically as if to say, "Why would you ask that?" Then she replies, "I told you, I doubt there are any left here."

"I guess they decided they wouldn't come back for the reunion," I answer lightly, trying to distract her from her nerves.

"*Grüss Gott!* Greetings," says the president of the reunion committee, Louis Goldenburgher, calling to attention the group of about twenty of my mother's grammar-school classmates. "A special greeting to Edith with all our hearts."

He is standing behind a podium at the center of several connecting tables that form a U. The room, decorated in a German fashion I've come to recognize, is filled with fifties-looking wooden tables and chairs, flags and seals on the walls, and a faux-brick linoleum floor. The tables, set for the coffee, feature an assortment of fancy German pastries and cakes, each perfectly decorated with evenly spaced fruits and peaks of whipped cream. A camera strobe flashes and I notice a photographer and a young reporter, probably from the *Darmstadter Echo*, standing in the back of the room.

"Edith, we're glad that you came back," Louis says to the group, whose eyes are fixed on him. "It is the first time in fifty-two years that we see each other. We thank you for returning, remembering your classmates, and visiting with us." When he pauses at the end of his sentences, an awkward silence speaks loudly of discomfort, chagrin, shame.

"We would like to welcome you and your daughter"—he looks over at my belly and smiles—"and your grandchild-to-be with these flowers." He strides over to our seats and presents each of us with a bouquet of red roses and baby's breath. "They came from the garden of our classmate Hilda Herz."

My mother has positioned her chair so that it is right up against mine, as if she desperately needs me next to her to get through this event. She is so close that I can hear her breathing through her nose. We both mutter an anxious *danke* as he returns to the podium. "Now, Edith, let me introduce you to the town's Bürgermeister, who would like to make a few remarks."

While the mayor moves to the front of the room, I scan the audience. No one looks directly at my mother or me; most sit in their chairs stiffly, knees pushed together, backs straight, and arms folded. No one says a word, so I notice sounds that normally would be lost in the noise of the room. Outside, the geese honk loudly. Inside, a chair leg scrapes across the floor.

"I welcome you in the name of the Town Council," the mayor begins, tensely, as Hans translates. He is a young man, probably in his early forties, one of those whom Hans calls a "*Spätgeborene*." The word, Hans says, is the label the Germans have given those too young to be held accountable for Nazi crimes. It means late-born. "We call them 'lucky-late-born,'" he says.

"Some years ago, my predecessor, the previous mayor, invited you to visit here. At that time, you declined the invitation, saying that you weren't ready to return to Stockstadt. We understood that. But now we are pleased that you came." He stops, drinks some water, and then continues.

"We hope that you feel at home here and comfortable talking to your classmates and the townspeople." A woman in her late forties, who is seated next to the mayor and is, I figure, his assistant, darts a quick glance at my mother and bites her lip to seal in her emotions. All the other classmates sit impassively, devoid of expression, without any affect.

"Many of us can well understand your remembrance of the past and the pain of those years. Now that you have been here a few days, we hope that you have had the chance to know us again." He stops, takes a deep breath, and continues. "We hope that this trip will give you a better feeling for your old home." Here, the mayor's assistant turns her eyes on my mother, loses her composure, and drapes her napkin over her face. Noticing this, the mayor pauses, clears his throat, and bucks himself up. "We hope . . . we hope that this new experience will stay with you and you will have different thoughts of Stockstadt.

"We want to present you with a few small gifts to remind you of your visit here. Please come up to the podium to accept them."

She gets up, awkwardly squeezes behind my chair to work her way toward him. He extends his hand to shake hers and says, "First, we're giving you this pewter plate with a linoleum engraving of a place we're sure you remember. It is the old Rathaus." He hands the plate to her, and as she says, *Danke*," she sets it in front of me so that I can see it. The Town Hall looks just as she described it, though the engraving is too small for the artist to record the storks' nest. The village church towers over the Rathaus, the cross at the top of the spire piercing white, billowy clouds.

"We hope it will be a nice remembrance for you of Stockstadt," the mayor continues. "In addition, we would like you to have this book about the area which shows you pictures from the past. Some of it will look very familiar to you. Some pictures will be unfamiliar, since they were taken more recently. . . . Well"—he stumbles—"what I mean is that they were taken within the last fifty years. I hope you will look at it at your leisure and be reminded of your travels here.

"We wish you a wonderful stay. We want you to enjoy being in Stockstadt again. Now we would like to hear a few words from you." He steps away from the podium to give her the floor.

"*Danke*," Mom begins, nervously. A diminutive figure behind the podium, she stretches to reach the microphone, but she doesn't adjust it to her level. Hans translates for me in calm tones that contrast sharply with the trembling, high-pitched voice in which she speaks German. "Thank you for the presents. It's good to see all of you again. It's interesting to be able to come here and look back."

I notice that she appears strikingly different from her classmates in her colorful, drop-waist silk dress and stylish heels. Unlike the men, who are wearing jackets and ties, the German women of her generation seem to give little thought to their appearance; most wear no makeup and are underdressed in dark pants and sweaters. In this context, my mother looks American; at home, she often looks German to me.

"Thank you for all the presents. I'm glad to have this chance to become reacquainted with the people who were my friends in school." She pauses to think of what to say next, then she blurts out, "We've all gotten older." The group titters, breaking some of the tension that has made the room feel as if we were about to witness an execution. When the audience quiets down, she adds, "It is special to me that you have celebrated my return. Thank you."

She quickly steps away from the podium as the group applauds politely. But before she can sit, a woman rushes toward her from the other side of the room, leans across the table, and says, "Do you remember me?" The woman has some sort of degenerative skin disorder which has spotted her face with red blotches. In addition, one of her eyes is much narrower than the other. I don't know how my mother would recognize her, even if she had seen her five years ago.

Dumbstruck, my mother obviously hasn't a clue. After a moment, the woman says, "I'm Ingrid Kraft."

My mother reaches over the table, grabs her around the neck, and hugs her, gently sobbing on the woman's shoulder.

"Of course I remember," Mom says. "How could I forget you?" My mother introduces her to me, but she, like everyone else here, speaks no English.

All I can do is smile, nod, and shake hands. For me, in this setting, the German language is itself a barrier: I cannot communicate with and so cannot know these people who shared a whole life with my mother. Even this close, they remain inaccessible to me. Here, the German language is like my mother's past, a room I cannot enter; I stretch even to peer through its windows to grasp some idea of what goes on within its walls.

Suddenly, several people are crowding around my mother and talking at once. Hans can't keep up with all of the strands of conversation. He translates as much as he can of my mother's interactions.

"Ingrid used to save a seat for me at the school," Mom explains to me, "even on Saturdays, the day I didn't go to school." They talk for a few moments about the schoolmate Ingrid married, her two children and what they do for a living, and how many grandchildren she has now.

After Ingrid returns to her seat, Mom whispers in my ear, "Ingrid saved me a seat long after it was acceptable. That's why I have such a special feeling for her. She saved me a seat even when the others teased me and made me feel uncomfortable."

Another woman sits in an empty chair next to Mom, grabs her elbow, and says, "I'm so glad you're here. There's something I always wanted to say to you. First, let me ask you. Do you know who I am?"

"I'm sorry," my mother says. "There are so many faces here and it was a long time ago." Then she turns to Hans and says, "I think I need a list of the classmates."

"I'm Berta Busch. We lived near the water. You may remember my family; we had very little money.

"Every year, a company would come and put up a Ferris wheel and carousel in the play space in front of your house. It was like a little carnival, but for the children it was a big event, something we all looked forward to every spring. Do you remember?"

"Yes, I remember," my mother says, bringing her hand up to her face and framing one eye as she tries to recall the scene.

"Because they used the Westerfeld property, the company gave your family free tickets. Do you remember?"

"Uh-huh," Mom says, "I remember that."

"I have never forgotten you because you gave me a very special memory. I couldn't afford to buy the tickets and I loved those rides. You knew that I couldn't buy them, so you gave me your tickets."

"I didn't remember that." Mom smiles, less tense now. "But I'm glad you did."

A man with a terrible limp lumbers across the room and approaches my mother, dipping from side to side with each step. When he reaches my mother, he says breathlessly, "I'm Karl Schumacher." He then tells her that he stepped on a mine during the war. "It was a terrible injury, very painful," he says. "I had many operations, but they could never make it right. I could not hold a job because of it.

"I don't know if you remember, Edith, but my parents did business with your family. I went with my father to your house to drop off crops and pick up supplies. I remember, every time I came to your house, your father would give me red candies. In fact, I think he handed them out to all the children. Is that right?"

"I'm not sure," she says. "I don't really remember that."

"I don't remember the red candies either," Berta says, "but I remember your Oma Sara sitting in front of your house as if it were yesterday. She would bring a chair into the play space and watch the children while she knitted or peeled potatoes for potato salad. Whenever a child passed her, Oma Sara would joke, '*Willst du eine Kartoffel essen?* Would you like a potato?' She was always there, always with the same line. For the children, she was almost an institution."

"Do you remember the sponges, Berta?" says Karl. "Back then, no one had any money and no one had any jobs. We were hungry and didn't even have money for things like shoes. Still, the school required that each child have certain supplies, including sponges to clean our chalkboards. But none of us could afford to buy them. Oma Sara said, 'I don't understand how you children can go to school and learn without one.' So she hand-knitted sponges for everyone in our class."

The mayor interrupts Schumacher and asks the classmates to sit down and have coffee. "Let's let Edith enjoy some of our food," he says. "We will talk and eat." Coffee is poured, cream and sugar are stirred into the cups, cakes are cut and served.

After we've taken a couple of bites and savored some of the pastries, a woman a few seats down from my mother says, "Do all of you remember when the Americans were here? I have such a happy memory of that time. One thing I can never forget is when they first came. Remember?" The woman turns to Louis, who is sitting next to her.

"Yes, Emma," he says. "Tell Edith about it."

"Well, as you may know, Stockstadt was a base for Americans. When a small platoon of American soldiers showed up, they saw a sea of white surrender flags. The entire town of Stockstadt came out and held flags. The soldiers thought the German platoon was so large that they couldn't take them on. So, for three days, they hesitated. When they finally came, the townspeople rejoiced that the Americans had arrived and they took them in as friends." With tears in her eyes, Emma says, "I still get goosebumps every time I think about that day."

"After they arrived," Louis adds, "many girls from the town of Stockstadt took up with the American soldiers. We lost a lot of women in the town to the Americans."

"Well," explains Emma, "we had nothing and the American soldiers seemed to have so much. So some girls who were a little older than us got involved and some got pregnant. We have quite a few children here who never met their American fathers. The soldiers would promise to send for the women after they returned home, but the women never heard from them again."

"Oh, really," my mother says animatedly. "Now that you mention it, I remember Marie Mund wrote me a letter around 1945. She asked me to please help her find an apartment in Chicago. She said that she was pregnant and the baby's father was an American who lived near Chicago. She wanted to move there in hopes of marrying the man. But I was so young then, and I really couldn't help her much. Do you know what happened to her?"

"She's still here," Emma says. "She had a son with the American, but

I don't think the boy ever met his father. She married another man and had two more children with him. But some women went to America and started a new life with these men. They rarely came home again." Then she elbows Louis and says, "You're still sore, aren't you, because you had a crush on an older girl and you lost her to an American."

"Oh." My mother tosses her head back and laughs.

"No, no," he says, waving his hand in denial. "I was so young then, what did I know? I'm sure it all worked out for the best—though, at the time, I was really heartbroken and furious that some stinky American stole my girl." Hans holds his nose to make Louis's point.

Laughter echoes through the group, as if they had forgotten themselves for a moment. But then they remember and the laughter stops immediately and the familiar, stilted silence sets in again. No one knows quite what to say. This time it is so prolonged that I almost expect someone to announce it's time to leave. Louis fiddles nervously with his spoon, clanging it against his coffee cup. Karl unconsciously rubs his thumb over the edge of the table through the tablecloth, and Emma gazes out the window at the geese.

Finally, she turns to my mother and says candidly, "Let us forget the bad things of the past. We were young and it was a long time ago."

"Yes," says a man sitting next to her. "We didn't even know what a concentration camp was." Here we go again, I think. *Wir haben nichts gewusst.* We knew nothing about this.

"We were children," Emma continues. "We did not think. We did what we were told."

I consider what she has said. "We did what we were told." Maybe, I think, this isn't just, "We knew nothing." Maybe this is a perspective I hadn't considered: Like my mother, they were twelve years old in 1938. They wouldn't know what concentration camps were, and even if they had heard of them, their parents probably denied that the camps existed. The children did what they were told to do—avoid and even castigate the Jews—no matter how misguided, hurtful, or wrong the behavior. Who were they to question their parents? Maybe they were late-born, too, though not so lucky.

"We witnessed terrible things," says Ingrid, dabbing her tears with her cloth napkin. "Edith, after you left, I thought of you often. I was so glad you were gone after 1938. You didn't have to see the cruelty of the Nazis. I saw things I can never forget. At least you didn't have to see the horrors and the abuse. At least you don't have to have those nightmares, too.

"There were so many victims," she continues. "My sister was one. They called her a collaborator because she worked for a Jewish family in the next town. She had to pay money and get affidavits to get work again." I think of Mina and wonder if she suffered for her association with the Westerfelds.

"Still," Ingrid says, "some so-called 'friends' refused to sign her papers. So she couldn't work for ten years because of her association with that family. Her life was very difficult."

"Yes, there were so many stories like that," says Karl Schumacher, the man with the terrible limp. "And so many others." He ponders that and then, after a moment, adds, "You know, you paid a terrible, terrible price because of the war. However, we paid a price, too. You were a victim. But in a different way, we were victims, too."

The talk turns lighter, more gossipy, and then winds down; it's clearly time for us to leave. My mother gets up to thank Louis and shake hands with the mayor and I nod and smile behind her. As we slowly make our way to the door, the whole crowd of about twenty-five people, including the reporters and the mayor's group, follow us down the corridor and out to the parking lot, where the red Rabbit waits for us.

"*Sehr schön Euch wieder zu sehen*. We were glad to see you," several people call out as we stand in a large circle near the car.

"*Es ist schön mit Euch gewesen*. It was nice to meet you again."

"*Komm wieder zurück*. Come back again."

But no one turns his or her back to leave. My mother doesn't seem to want to get in the car yet. She leans against the Rabbit's door and repeats her goodbyes, reiterating the same sentiments over and over.

"*Sehr schön mit Euch zu treffen*," I hear from my mother and the others again.

Impatiently, Hans and I look at each other as if to say, "Let's go." But neither one of us wants to interrupt her or rush her. I hang back and take in the odd scene. Fifty-two years earlier, many of those in this group may have taunted her or shunned her in the classroom. And I'm sure there were many other painful incidents. Yet now she doesn't want to leave; she can't bring herself to part with them.

Finally, the prolonged, reluctant goodbye seems almost absurd, even to my mother, and she turns to me and says, "I suppose we should go."

"I suppose so," I say, making my way around to the driver's side.

She opens the passenger's door, hugs the nearest classmates, and calls out, "*Auf Wiedersehen*." She climbs into the passenger seat and cracks the window to call out one last "*Auf Wiedersehen*." We pull away, but she continues to wave through the window until they are out of view.

When we are several blocks away from the reunion, my mother turns around in her seat and says to Hans, "The whole time we were there, I was wondering why Gretel Klingler didn't come. Did you talk to her?"

"Yes, I called her and told her about the reunion," Hans says vaguely. "But she said she wouldn't be able to make it."

"Really, I'm disappointed," my mother says. "I used to save a seat for her at school every day. I really wanted to see her again. I wonder why she didn't come."

She turns that over in her mind and then adds, "From the way they talked, it sounded like these annual reunions are the high point of their social season and no one likes to miss them."

"When you called," I ask Hans, "did she say why she couldn't come?"

"No, not really," he says, obviously uncomfortable. "She just said she wouldn't make it."

"Tell me," I ask, "how many of my mother's classmates are still alive but decided not to attend the reunion?"

"Ohhh, I don't know really," he says.

I know he knows, but he doesn't want to say. "Well, how many people told you they couldn't come today?"

He hesitates. Maybe he's counting in his head. Finally, he concedes, "I'd say eight or so."

"Eight. Out of twenty-eight in the class?" I ask. "Is that right?"

"Yes," he says. "I suppose that's right."

Chapter 9

*I*t's a bright, sunny Thursday morning and Hans has invited us to his house so we can see his garden. After a late start, we drive a few blocks from the hotel to a quaint, humble neighborhood of one- and two-bedroom homes, nothing older than twenty years or so. Hans's house stands out, surrounded as it is by the last colorful geraniums, impatiens, mums, and roses of the season. This impressive carpet of blooms is broken only by the occasional landscape ornament.

After we've admired his flowers, Hans asks us to come inside. We enter a dark, narrow hallway in his small house. He briefly introduces us to his wife, Alice, an attractive woman in her sixties. Dressed unpretentiously in slacks and a golf shirt, her gray hair casual in a shoulder-length bob, she stands in the kitchen doorway and greets us with great warmth in broken English.

"Velcome, velcome home," she says, smiling. I think she means, Welcome to *our* home. "Good you here."

Hans leads us into the living room, but Alice doesn't follow. Instead, as if on cue, she excuses herself, and a moment later, I hear her clanging pots.

The modest living room feels like an extension of Hans's second-floor museum. Artifacts that didn't fit there fill this room's floor-to-ceiling shelves in a jumbled, helter-skelter fashion. Worn glass bottles, musty books, skulls, arrowheads, even old hats clutter the dark room, making it feel smaller than it is.

In contrast, tidy and spare, are the burning memorial candles arranged on a bureau next to the pictures of Hans's dead son. The sweet smell of the candles' incense suffuses the room.

"I have something for you today," he says solemnly, rubbing the back of his neck as if it aches. "Please sit down." He points to a crowded seating area. Barely able to squeeze my knees between the coffee table and the couch, off-balance from my belly, I stumble and rattle the cups on the table. I flop backward onto the overstuffed couch, blushing with embarrassment. Hans, tense and preoccupied this morning, doesn't notice; my mother's back is to me as she looks at the pictures on the bureau. I'm just relieved to be seated.

I look at the coffee table and realize that everything is all prepared, as if Hans had premeditated the setting. A coffeepot, a water pitcher, fine cups and fancy glasses, plates, spoons, cloth napkins, and pastries in a wire basket are neatly arranged on a tray in the center of the coffee table. Next to the coffeepot on the tray is a carefully folded copy of the *Darmstadter Echo*. When I see the paper's banner, my stomach takes a precipitous, anxious dive.

Hans sets himself stiffly on the edge of a slipcovered armchair opposite the couch and then exhales a tense, shallow sigh. My mother, banging her knees just like me, settles down on the couch next to me.

"I want to translate an article for you that appeared in today's paper," he says in a rehearsed, taut voice. "It's very important to me that we read it together . . . out loud."

He pours us each a cup of coffee, offers cream and sugar, then picks up the paper. "I will read it in German and then translate it for you into English," he says. He pours himself a tall glass of ice water and then snaps open the paper. My mother and I exchange a nervous, quick glance, unsettled by the careful arrangement of this scene.

"*Unvergessliche Begegnung mit Stockstädter Jüdin*" is the headline of the story, meaning "Unforgettable Meeting with a Jew of Stockstadt."

"Here's what the story says: *Jahrhundert in Stockstadt gelebt hatten, nur noch zwei; die Familien Westerfeld und Kahn. . . .* At the turn of the century, two Jewish families lived in Stockstadt—the Kahns and the Westerfelds," he begins, his voice a note higher than usual. "In 1891, Siegmund Westerfeld was born in his family home in Stockstadt. During the 1920s, he opened his own business in that house, selling meat and seeds for the farmers to the market. Today, at the same point a different business flourishes. It is a kiosk selling liquor and magazines.

"Still, whenever town historian Hans Hermann walks past the new business, he always thinks about the old business that Westerfeld ran there. Hermann remembers that his father bought food for the pigs at the Westerfeld house. He remembers seeing the local farmers bringing cows to the house so that Westerfeld could bring them to market. He remembers seeing Siegmund unloading wagons full of produce into the shop. He even remembers small things. For example, he says that on the left side of the shop Westerfeld put sacks of feed. On the right, shelves were stocked with preserved goods. In the house, the Westerfelds had one of the first telephones in the town."

Hans pauses, licks his lips, and then continues. "In 1935, SS men from Stockstadt started to threaten the Westerfelds and their customers. It got so bad that Siegmund was beaten up in the middle of the street. Nobody did anything to resist the Nazis or help the Westerfelds. The t-t-townspeople," he stutters, "the townspeople all . . . all looked the other way." Hans's voice trails off at the end of this sentence.

He stops again, collects himself. Hans seems compelled to do this reading, but I wonder whether he'll be able to get through it. His voice shakes and the newspaper crackles in his trembling hands. He can hardly hold it still so that he can read. I hear the words he said to me at his son's grave: *I know what you want to know, but it is very delicate. I will tell you the truth when I'm ready.*

He doesn't really seem ready now; but then Hans finds his voice again. "Westerfeld went to the Lord Mayor and the Assembly to complain, but he got no sympathy. When he left the Town Hall, the farmers beat him up again and threw him down the two-story staircase. Many farmers owed Westerfeld a lot of money since Westerfeld often extended credit to them. The farmers didn't come to Westerfeld's aid because they didn't want to pay off their debts.

"The terror against the two families became worse and worse." Hans is translating more slowly now; he comes to a stop and takes several sips of water. Then he perseveres. "Moses Kahn, the grandfather of the other Jewish family in town, sensed what was happening. He took Siegmund Westerfeld aside and told him that the Kahns were going to start a new life in America. Kahn wanted Westerfeld to persuade the family to leave, too. Westerfeld said he couldn't do that because his mother, Sara, would rather die than leave. She insisted that she was born a German and would always remain a German. Westerfeld wouldn't go without his mother.

"But the Westerfelds decided to send their daughters, who were then twelve and fifteen, to America. In 1937, the Jewish Children's Bureau helped place Betty in a home near Chicago. A year later, Edith went to live with an aunt and uncle, also in Chicago. Before leaving, the girls pleaded with their parents to join them in America, but the Westerfelds said they were too old to start over. They didn't believe that the Germans would do them any harm.

"On November 9, 1938, there was to be the pogrom called Kristallnacht. In Stockstadt, everything was calm. But in the bright daylight of November 10, a troop of black-shirted fascists from Darmstadt stormed the house of the Westerfelds.

"Siegmund, Sara, and Frieda—" Now Hans breaks down; tears roll down his face. He fights to regain his composure, but he can't collect himself. Several moments pass. He straightens the paper, swallows to regain his voice, and finally continues reading.

"Siegmund, Sara, and Frieda sat on the street curb with their hands in their faces and cried as the Nazis destroyed their home. For a half-hour, the Nazis raided the Westerfeld home and threw things out of the windows—dishes, clothes, lamps, silver, clocks, linens, toys, mirrors, pictures, candelabras, even furniture like chairs, dressers, and beds. Half the village stood in a large semicircle in front of the house, in the space where the children once played. The townspeople just stood there watching." Again Hans pauses, takes several deep breaths, then presses forward.

"Some stood in shock with their mouths open. They knew they couldn't do anything. They feared for their own lives. But others stood there smiling.

"'I was sixteen years old then and remember that I was disgusted,' explains Hermann. 'But I didn't know how to react. I didn't know if I should react. I was torn.'

"After this day, when the Westerfelds lost the last things they owned, they could no longer live in Stockstadt. The townspeople boycotted the Westerfeld business; they had no opportunity to earn money. So the Westerfelds were left with no choice but to sell their home and move to Darmstadt. There, Siegmund worked for a while in a Jewish furniture store where he had had a job during college.

"A few years later, in 1942, Hermann was a volunteer to the Marines. He was naïve and proud of his uniform. One day, he was strutting through the streets of Darmstadt in his uniform when he came upon Frieda. By this time, Siegmund was already in concentration camp and she was living in an apartment for Jews that SS soldiers guarded.

"Hermann noticed Frieda first and saw that she had grown old and gray since the last time he saw her, though she was only forty-two years old. She was wearing a nice navy dress frayed from wear. It had a yellow star on the front and back. When Frieda recognized Hermann, she reached for him, hugged him, and started to cry. This was extremely dangerous, since a decree in October of 1941 made 'friendly relations of any kind with Jews punishable by imprisonment.'

"She cried to Hermann that they had taken Siegmund to a concentration camp near Berlin called Sachsenhausen. She was desperate.

"'Please help me,' she begged. 'Please, please. You can do something. You must. I was your neighbor, your friend. I watched you grow up.' But Hermann says he was overcome with angst and fear."

Hans stops cold, paralyzed by emotion. He drops the paper in his lap, places his hands over his eyes in grief and shame. The entire room is charged. His story mesmerizes me, but I can hardly bear to watch him, to listen to another moment of his torment. Part of me wants to ask him to stop.

"All right, Hans," my mother says softly, swallowing hard and waving her hand to say that he doesn't have to go on. "It was a long time ago. Forget it."

He wipes his eyes with his sleeve. "I can't," he says. After a long pause, he says again, "I can't. I can't forget."

The uncomfortable silence grows longer and longer, at last prodding Hans to begin reading again.

"He was frightened to be in this situation. He knew he couldn't help her.

"'I . . . I put my hands up,'" Hans slowly chokes through the words, "'and . . . and . . . and turned away without saying a word.'"

He stops for several seconds, stares at the page, never looking up at my mother. "This event with Frieda," he continues, "has haunted him for his whole life. She was in such bad circumstances and he didn't help her in her moment of need. He never saw her again.

"Siegmund died of hunger in concentration camp in 1941. For several years, Hermann says, the Town Hall kept a sign posted on its bulletin board announcing Siegmund's death. He went every week to check the board to see if there was news about Frieda, but there never was. No one knows for sure what became of her. Many think she died in a concentration camp in Poland. Hermann remained a volunteer through the end of the war.

"Just a few days ago, the past came alive again for Hermann. An American woman, Edith Schumer, came to Stockstadt and claimed she was a Westerfeld. The Town Hall officials immediately called Hermann because he is the keeper of the records and they thought he might like to talk to her about her life and early German experience.

"Hans felt he needed to spend the week with Edith and her daughter to share the past and the history of the family. But, during the week, a lot of hurts came up again. He felt he owed them more than his time; he owed them some explanation. So he asked the *Darmstadter Echo* to write a story on his experience. He wanted the newspaper to tell his story so that he could admit his role in the past.

"'I wanted Edith Westerfeld, her daughter, and all of Stockstadt to know what really happened,'" Hans says with finality. "*Wir sind mit ihr verbunden—wir haben nichts gemacht*. We became bound to her because we did nothing."

By now, so many emotions flood me that I sob just for some sort of release. As I dig in my purse for a tissue, I notice that the hairs on my arms stand on end. Then I look at my mother, and to Hans. All of us are weeping and sniffling and we catch each other's gaze. But none of us touch or hug. No one can talk; we're each alone with our grief.

Then my mother—oddly, the most composed of the three of us—asks him directly: "Are you asking for my forgiveness?"

"No." He clears his throat and adds, "No, I don't think so. I just . . . I just wanted you to know.

"I guess," he says after some thought, "your forgiveness doesn't really matter." His emotions well up, blocking in his throat. "Because I'll never forgive myself. Even if I want to, I can't."

His sleeve blots another batch of tears. "I've learned to live with it, I suppose, just as you have. But it's always with me."

"Every night of my life, before I go to sleep, I see an image of your mother in that dress with the yellow star," he says quietly. "Or I see me, swaggering in that uniform. Or I feel myself put up my hands, almost instinctively, automatically, without any thought. I feel myself turn away from her. Over and over again."

Again, he takes a deep breath. "I suppose that is my punishment," he says, matter-of-factly, as if he had come to terms with it a long time ago.

"I am forever condemned by my memory."

Chapter 10

"I'm not going to be able to come with you to see Mina today," Hans says, as we pull up to his house just before noon Friday.

After a late start, we are about to set out to try to find Mina's sanitarium in the Odenwald Mountains. We had expected Hans to come along, but now, as he leans into the passenger's window, we can see he doesn't look well. Dark circles ring his eyes; maybe he did not sleep last night. The line between his eyebrows cuts a deep crease, as if he has buried a worry deep in it; today, he looks old.

"Gee," Mom says, in a disheartened tone, "I'm disappointed. I was looking forward to it. I thought you might be able to show us some sights outside Stockstadt that I never got to see."

"I'm sorry," he says, casting a downward glance. He doesn't seem himself. Maybe he is uncomfortable with what he revealed yesterday; maybe he said too much and feels exposed. Or maybe he doesn't want to see Mina. Ever since Mom first mentioned her name, I've seen that something about her troubles him, that she somehow has planted her-self in his consciousness, so that the mere sound of her name makes him squirm.

"Something has come up," he adds anxiously. "I just can't make it, but I've made a map for you." He reaches into the inside pocket of his jacket and pulls out three pages of directions and hand-drawn maps, all elabo-rately delineated with colored pens. Obviously, he spent quite a bit of time preparing these.

"The little village shouldn't be too hard to find," he explains. "When you get to a neighboring town, go to the local pub and ask for directions to her house. They'll know where she lives. Tell them the bed and break-fast is in the town of Tromm in Grasellenbach."

"When do you think you'll return to Stockstadt?" he asks in closing.

"I don't know," Mom says.

"Well, call me when you're at the hotel again," he says, backing away from the car. He waves dismissively. "Drive carefully, and have a good trip."

"Thanks," Mom calls as she rolls up the window. Hans, having practi-cally sprinted back to his house, is in the front doorway already.

Picturesque, quaint, romantic: these are the words I would use if I sent my family a postcard from the Odenwald Mountains. Clearly, this is a vacation spot for Germans, though it's far less commercialized than its American counterparts, such as Martha's Vineyard or Door County, Wisconsin.

Still, each town has its tourist patch, a couple of shops selling sou-venirs and trinkets. Just past each town, the landscape returns to scenes of greenish-yellow vineyards planted on steep mountains; fences ex-actly three feet apart frame the perfectly straight lines of vines. The sloping yellow mountain looks like a magnified view of a caterpillar's back.

We must be getting closer to Mina's remote town. As Hans sug-gested, we find the next pub to ask for directions to the village of Tromm.

"No," the bartender shakes his head. "Never even heard of it."

"Have you ever heard of Mina Fiedler's Inn?" my mother asks.

"No. No." He shakes his head and shrugs his shoulders.

"Now what?" I ask Mom, as we get back into the car.

"Let's drive in the same direction to the next town and see if they know where Tromm is."

We try again, but get the same response. No one has heard of Tromm, no one knows of Mina. We're heading deeper into the country, each town a greater distance from the last. The views are living post-cards of a rural Europe that tourists don't always see. The car windows frame fleeting pictures of vineyards, sheep, cows, rugged mountains, wide blue skies, and endless evergreen forests. Only an occasional farm-house suggests humans in the landscape.

We drive another ten miles or so. Now, I notice, some signs tell us how many kilometers to towns in other countries, like Zurich.

"Mom, I think we've gone too far," I say. "We've been driving over two and a half hours, and according to Hans's maps, it should only take an hour and a half. We took a few wrong turns, but that ate up only fif-teen minutes." Hans's maps are crumpled and torn, their colorful mark-ings smeared in my mother's sweaty hands after hours of her clutching and studying them.

"This seems hopeless," I say. "I wonder if we'll ever find her."

"We will," Mom says. "I'm not giving up. She would never forgive me if she knew we were here and didn't find her. Let's ask at the next town."

"That could be a while," I say with undisguised exasperation. We drive another twenty minutes and finally see a sign for Grasellenbach, the area Hans mentioned.

"*Wo ist Tromm?*" my mother asks the bartender at the next pub. He di-rects us, saying it's just a few miles from here. However, when Mom asks if he knows Mina Fiedler, he tells her he has lived here for fifteen years, knows almost everyone in the area, but has never heard her name. "If she lives in Tromm," he says, "she doesn't get many visitors."

When at last we find the town, it's obvious why only the closest neighbors know it's here. Tromm consists of five houses tucked off a remote road at the top of a mountain. A restaurant, the only commercial enterprise here, occupies the first floor of one of the houses.

"Which house do you think is Mina's?" my mother asks.

"I have no idea," I say. "Let's knock on this door." As I pull into the driveway of the first house, I notice that the sun is no longer high in the sky and the light is ebbing.

A woman answers and tells us that Mina lives next door, pointing to the dilapidated Tudor house across from her property. Next to it is an even more dilapidated wing of rooms into which part of the wood-shingled roof has collapsed.

This must be the Inn, but obviously no one has recuperated here, or even opened the doors to the rooms, in decades. It's uninhabitable, I think. It probably ought to be condemned.

We knock on the front door of the house, but no one answers. The sound of a radio blares inside the house. My mother raps again. No answer. Carved into the tightly closed gray shutters are waning crescent moons that face each other; the house is dark.

"It doesn't look like anyone's home," I say.

"But the radio is on," Mom says.

She raps again, louder. No answer. "Maybe we should go around and knock at the side door," I say.

We take a few steps toward the other door—but stop when, suddenly, a second-floor shutter rattles and scrapes under the unaccustomed pressure of opening. An old woman pokes her head out and stares. Her long, thin white hair is piled tidily on top of her head; an unbecoming pair of glasses hides her eyes, and a thick, old-fashioned gray dress and maroon cardigan cover the rest of her.

"*Was ist das?*" she says suspiciously.

"Can that be Mina?" my mother, wide-eyed, whispers to me. "She was a beautiful girl with long, thick, wavy blond hair that she braided and pinned up. She's so old."

Mom looks at the woman again and then tentatively, almost deferentially, calls her by name: "*Mina?*"

The woman looks bewildered. "*Ja?*" she replies warily.

"*Ich bin Edith. Edith Westerfeld.*"

For a long moment, the woman stares intently at my mother but says nothing. Then she starts to quiver; the shutter she clutches in her hand now groans as she leans on it for support. Breathing heavily, she thumps a flat palm on her chest, trying to calm her heart. "*Ich komme schnell 'runter.* I'll be right down," she cries, then she struggles to close and lock the shutter.

In seconds, Mina swings open the side door and breathlessly lunges toward my mother, capturing her in a fervent hug. She holds her tight and won't let her go. "Tiddy," she says, tears of joy springing from her eyes, "Tiddy."

She is breathing heavily, coughing between her words; her rush of emotion seems to have caused some sort of respiratory seizure, perhaps an asthma attack, yet she is oblivious to everything but my mother.

"*Ich hab' nicht gedacht, dass ich dich wiedersehen werde,*" they murmur together. "I never thought I'd see you again," Mom says.

The two survey each other at arm's distance, hug again, mutter loving exchanges in German, moan, over and over again. "*Ich bin so froh dich wieder zu sehen.* I'm so happy to see you again." Mina hacks in my mother's ear, but refuses to let her go.

I hover in the doorway, watching them. I notice that Mina wears a pair of old handmade slippers over slightly unmatched blue socks folded around the ankle; she has crocheted red yarn into the holes in the cardboard soles. Some of the holes have broken so that the socks show through.

"*Es ist schon eine lange Zeit her, Tiddy.* It's been so long, Tiddy," Mina says. The lump rises in my throat, and I wonder about the name Mina calls my mother, "Tiddy." What could that mean?

"Ohhhhh," Mina gasps suddenly, interrupting their moving reunion, as she realizes that she left a pan cooking on the stove. We follow her into a cluttered, dark cave of a kitchen, crowded with a round-edged refrigerator, a 1930s stove on legs, and an old sink whose plumbing consists of a goose-necked pipe exposed underneath. Dirty dishes encrusted with food totter on the ridged, yellowed porcelain that stretches to the left of the sink. A distinct smell of cat urine permeates the room.

Mina had been heating milk before we knocked and, in the excitement, completely forgot about it. As I walk past the stove, the scalded milk and blackened aluminum pan produce yet another rank odor.

"What's 'Tiddy'?" I ask my mother as Mina shuts off the gas, grabs the handle with a torn, old kitchen towel, and places the pan and towel in the sink.

" 'Tiddy' was the name I called myself when I was two or so, before I could say 'Edith,' " my mother explains. "It stuck and became my nickname. Everyone in my family—my mother and father, my sister and Mina—called me 'Tiddy.' "

As Mina runs water into the pan in the sink, we have a moment to look around. Papers, magazines, and books are piled in wobbly towers around the room. A bare, glaring light bulb hangs above the center of a worn, deeply scarred wooden table on which a couple of old sleepy cats are curled comfortably, quite uninterested in the visitors. Several baskets and bags crammed with clothing, pictures, and papers crowd the floor, making it difficult to walk in her kitchen.

She must save everything, I think, even old newspapers; they're covering the floor and some of her furniture. Mina appears to be a recluse, a bag lady with a home.

"*Setz dich hin*," Mina says, pointing to the pressed-back chairs at the kitchen table where she wants us to sit. More folded newspapers cover the seats, and I hesitate; my mother is busy telling Mina that I am her *Tochter*, her daughter, but I stand, not knowing whether I should remove the paper or sit on top of it.

Then Mina sits, causing the paper on her chair to crackle loudly. I sit, too, and immediately realize why the paper is there: for support in the spots where the caning in the seat has worn through.

She opens a gold-and-white plastic cloth that had been folded on half of the table. Then she reaches with her greenish-veined, age-spotted hand, to grasp my smooth palm as her blue eyes seize my own dark gaze; I am fixed in her sight, I cannot move or look away. I am stuck to her like skin to dry ice.

"*Sie sieht aus wie deine Mutter*," Mina says, and my mother translates, "She looks just like your mother." Mina closes her eyes as if to picture my grandmother, to be certain her evaluation is fair and correct. Suddenly, a sure knowledge sweeps me: this moment, with this confusing and ancient woman, is as close as I will ever get to being in the company of my grandmother.

As Mina clutches my right hand, I point to the rose-gold ring I wear, the one my mother brought from Germany and gave me when my son was born. "Do you remember my grandmother's ring?" I ask her as my mother translates.

She examines the ring for a brief moment. "*Das ist nicht der Ring deiner Grossmutter*. That's not your grandmother's ring," she says firmly, a little annoyed that I have the wrong information. "That belonged to your great-grandmother, Oma Sara." She turns over my hand, examines the band, and adds, "And you had it made smaller."

She's right, but I'm amazed she remembers my great-grandmother's ring, let alone its size.

"What's the date today?" Mina asks, as if something just popped into her head. She strains to turn around, eyebrows arched as she looks at a calandar hanging on the wall, and asks, "Is it still the first week of October?"

"*Ja*," my mother replies. "It's October 5."

"How strange," she says, her eyes narrowing in an eerie look. "How strange that you should come to me this week."

"Why is that?" my mother asks.

"It's the week your father, Herr Westerfeld, died," she says, as if she keeps the Jewish custom of lighting a jahrzeit candle to mark the anniversary of a loved one's death. "It was forty-nine years ago. He died on October 3, 1941, in Sachsenhausen.

"*Schweinehunde!*" she spits fiercely. My mother says she's referring to the Nazis, calling them something like swine-dogs.

"Do you realize," Mina resumes as Mom translates, "that when your father died those *Schweinehunde* posted a sign in the Rathaus for over a year saying '*Jude Gestorben.*' *Sie machen mich krank.* 'Jew Died.' They make me sick."

She starts to cough uncontrollably and struggles for breath, placing both hands on her chest in a useless gesture toward relieving this awful asthma attack. I feel as if I were watching her strangle, as if some weight on her chest were crushing the breath right out of that thin body, its gasping and wheezing worsening with each breath. As she hacks, she stretches across the table for the inhaler that's just out of her reach. A look of panic crosses my mother's face as she dives for the inhaler, grabs it, and hands it to Mina. My mother lovingly places her left hand on Mina's shoulder and, with her right, steadies Mina's hand so she can aim several squirts of the medication into her mouth. Mina closes her eyes, which now look sunken, as she deeply inhales the vapor. Distress and worry alter the landscape of my mother's face. Mina sprays again and the coughing subsides a little. Finally, after a few long, frightening moments, the coughing stops.

"*Schweinische Leute*," Mina growls, picking up exactly where she left off; her eyes burn with a roaring fire. Mom, obviously much more alarmed than Mina over the asthma attack, has barely calmed down. She perches herself tentatively at the edge of her seat, ready to attend to Mina, never taking her eyes off her patient.

"What's *schweinische Leute*?" I ask Mom.

"What?" she asks, obviously having missed a few beats. "Oh, it means 'swine people,' or something like that."

Suddenly, I recognize Mina as Miss Havisham in *Great Expectations*, a woman barricaded in a dismal house where, in her mind, all the clocks stopped nearly fifty years ago. She is stuck in a time, arrested, wedded to her cause.

In the next moment, Mina's fury gives way to mourning as she begins to rock slowly from side to side in grief. "*Er war gerade wie ein Vater zu mir*," she says softly, closing her eyes and beginning to sob. "He was like a father to me." She takes out a hankie from the sleeve of her dress, lifts her glasses, revealing two white, oily depressions on each side of her nose, and soaks up her tears.

I hesitate to disrupt her reverie, but I have so many questions and I know we won't have much time together. "How is it that you lived with my mother's family?" I ask.

"You see"—she comes back, collecting herself to answer—"I came from very little. It was a big, working-class family, very poor, very unhappy. They trudged through life every day. They handled each other roughly. When things got really bad, they couldn't afford to feed me, so they asked the Westerfelds if I could live with them in exchange for work."

"Mina was with us five or six years," my mother adds. "By living with us, she had a much better life."

"That's right," Mina continues. "I came from nothing. I remember one year my parents gave me a little chocolate rabbit for Easter. To me, that was really something, because we never had chocolate or any treat.

"But at your house, there was food and even treats. Even better, I was appreciated. I liked to work. I loved the kids. I had a family." She thinks about that for a moment and then adds, "The years I spent with the Westerfelds were some of the best in my life."

She stops, looks off distantly, then turns to my mother with a smile and asks, "*Tust du noch an die alten Zeiten denken, Tiddy?* Do you remember those times, Tiddy? *Tust du noch an die alten Zeiten denken?* Do you remember?"

My mother looks away from Mina at the cat on the table. "He has such a bushy tail," my mother tells Mina, running a closed fist along the length of the cat's tail. "And it's so soft."

Mina, ignoring my mother's digression, rephrases her question: "You couldn't have forgotten, could you?" My mother doesn't respond to Mina. "*Tust du noch an die alten Zeiten denken, Tiddy?* Do you remember those times, Tiddy?"

"Somewhat," she says faintly, scratching the cat under its chin; she's still more engaged by the cat than by Mina.

"Wait right here," Mina says. She gets up and leaves the room. We hear her banging drawers and cabinets. After a few minutes she returns, her arms filled with old envelopes, pictures, and papers—her world in scraps, shoved and stuffed into tattered yellow envelopes.

"This ought to help you remember." She puts the pile on the table and starts rifling through an envelope of pictures. She pulls out a photograph and shows it to me first, pointing to the people and identifying each: "Tiddy, Betty, Mina, Frieda, and Siegmund."

A revelation: Frieda, my grandmother, is smiling. Here is the only picture I've ever seen in which she smiles, her impish grin transforming a face I have known only as careworn and frightened. At last, and for the very first time, I see the resemblance between my grandmother and me.

"Ohhh, those days were something," Mina says, handing the photo to my mother. She glances at it quickly, then returns it to the pile. "Remember how you used to jump into my arms after school, before even greeting your Oma? Ohhh, how that annoyed her. Oma could be a real czar and she would get so hurt and jealous because you didn't go to her first.

"Do you remember how you would wrap your arms and legs around me when I sat on the stool to milk the cows? Sometimes," she says, giggling, "I would lose my balance and we would both tumble onto the ground. Remember, once we made such a fuss that the cow tried to kick us."

Mina bombards my mother with questions and memories, but my mother resists engaging in the conversation. I know my mother wants to be here, but she isn't quite ready to face all that Mina presents.

This woman remembers everything; she has seared dates, images, and details into her brain. To secure her memories, she has kept every shred of evidence, each picture, any note that proves that the past happened. She turns a spotlight on her remembrances, while my mother keeps hers dimly lit, if not dark. For Mina the past is alive, not fossilized, as it is for my mother.

She talks of the games my mother, my Aunt Betty, and she played as children, of the times they laughed over something that only children would find funny. She animatedly recalls a weekend when my mother, after a brief stay at a cousin's house in the next town, called Mina to pick her up on the bicycle. Mina even remembers the smallest details, like the old red-checkered pillow she brought so little Tiddy's bottom wouldn't get sore as she rode on the back of the bike.

Now she bubbles with more old stories, hoping to jog my mother's memory. But Mom seems guarded; she continues to pet the cat and occasionally looks up at Mina with glassy eyes, intent but distant, as if she were listening to someone describe highlights of a television show she hadn't seen.

Suddenly, Mina stops smiling; a gloomy cloud rolls in unexpectedly, threatening and darkening her spirit. "*Ich kann das nicht vergeben*. I cannot forgive them. There are so many things that I can never forgive," she says angrily. "It wasn't just the crimes they committed. It's how they changed my life; they interrupted my childhood; stole our happy times.

"*An was erinnerst du dich noch*? What is it you remember?" Mina asks my mother urgently. Mom looks away again.

"You must remember something," Mina prods.

"I . . . I do," my mother responds after a long pause. She bites her lip. "I wish . . . I wish I remembered the happy things like you. Instead, the bad things that happened before I left have stayed with me."

"Ahhh, I remember those things, too," Mina says, and then adds sympathetically, "*Die sind sehr schwer zu vergessen*. They are hard to forget." Tears choke my mother as she looks for comfort in the deep blue of Mina's eyes. The two hold hands across the corner of the table, without saying anything. My mother tilts her head back, closes her eyes, as, I suppose, she replays old scenes. Mina searches her face for a glimmer of a shared memory.

Finally, my mother looks directly at Mina and inhales deeply. A tremor takes her voice when she says, "I remember . . . I remember when Betty took mandolin lessons and gave a recital with four boys." She looks wounded.

"*Ja*," Mina says, knowingly nodding her head. "That was the beginning . . . the beginning of all the troubles for your family."

"What happened?" I ask. "What was the incident?"

"The night of the recital," Mina explains, "Müller, the town's biggest Nazi and the Bürgermeister, was in the audience. He didn't like having a Jew perform. So he made the music teacher stop giving Betty lessons. That was the first time the Nazis in Stockstadt restricted what the Jews could do. Soon after, they said no more practicing gymnastics with the other children or using the school playground equipment.

"*Ach*, please." Mina takes her hand from my mother's and waves in disgust. She clears her throat with another cough. My mother leans on an elbow with a hand covering her mouth and her eyes downcast. "After that, there were so many rules and so many incidents."

"What else do you remember?" I ask.

"*Alles*. Everything. Everything," Mina whispers for emphasis. She stares at me hauntingly and then looks up at the bare bulb above the table in an effort to check the tears spilling from her eyes.

"For me, it feels like . . . it feels like it all happened yesterday. I remember everything." But she seems to want to remember everything, as if through memory she is consoled. She preserves the people and the past so she can hold on to them; it is her way of keeping the Westerfelds alive.

When she has collected herself, she turns to my mother again. "And, Tiddy, remember when the community wouldn't let you swim in the area in the Rhein sectioned off for public swimming. They put up a sign, oh, around 1935, that said, '*Juden sind hier nicht erwünscht*. Jews not wanted here.'

"This was terrible. If you couldn't go to the pool, there was nothing to do all summer. So remember, Tiddy? I dug a little pool in the yard and we played in it."

"Yes," Mom says, coming around a little. "I remember what you said to me then." She pauses, looks at Mina lovingly with her bottomless brown eyes. "You told me, '*Wenn sie dich nicht gehen lassen, will ich auch nicht gehen*. If they won't let you go, I won't go there either.'" She looks off distantly, and then adds softly, "You can't imagine what that meant to me."

Focusing on Mina again, she says ardently, "In that moment, I felt nothing could come between us . . . nothing. We were true sisters."

"*Ja*," Mina agrees. "*Ja, wahre Schwestern*. True sisters." Those German words echo in my ears as the three of us sit quietly. With her thumb, Mina plays with the corner of a picture on the table while my mother watches.

"So that summer," Mina continues, "we splashed in our backyard pool and made our own good time.

"If only we could have gotten around them that easily," she adds, and then goes on to describe some ways the Nazis pressured her. Often, her classmates taunted her for living with the Jews, and she lost her weekend housekeeping job after she and a friend were caught making fun of all the signs around town warning "*Juden*" not to do this and that.

"'Have you eaten any Jews today?' we laughed," Mina explains. "Müller heard us and he said, 'He who laughs loudest, won't have the last laugh.'" Then, she says, Müller forced the family not to hire her anymore.

"Müller was the worst of the *Schweinehunde*," she says, coughing again. Any mention of Nazis seems to irritate Mina's throat. "But there were others, too."

She removes her glasses and sets them on top of a newspaper on the table. The angle from where I'm sitting gives me a view through her bifocal lenses; the black ink of the newsprint is large, distorted, and fuzzy, like an oversized, terrifying insect.

Mina rubs the bridge of her nose, feeling for something. "Do you remember how I got this?" Mina points to a white, slightly indented scar, maybe a half-inch long.

"Sort of," Mom says. "A rock, right?"

"A couple of weeks before you left," Mina says, straightening her glasses on her nose, "some Nazis broke windows in the house with rocks in the middle of the night. While I was sleeping, a shard of glass cut me right here.

"The following Saturday night, a fellow asked me to dance at the Town Hall. I told him, 'I won't dance with you because you threw rocks at our house.' He said, 'Too bad it didn't kill you.'

"Just after that incident, they sent Tiddy away," she says with heaviness. Her voice breaks as she murmurs, "*Das war mein traurigster Tag. That was my saddest day.*" She puts a hand on her forehead and swallows. Mom takes her other hand and then reaches for her elbow to hug her. Mina's head rests on my mother's shoulder, her eyes closed tightly. When Mina sits back in her chair, large teardrops pool into her glasses, then slosh onto her dress. Seeing this, my mother picks up Mina's hand and gently massages the greenish veins and brown age spots.

"When Tiddy left"—she removes her hand to take off her glasses and dry them with a tissue—"*ein Stückchen von meinem Herz war mitgenommen.* She took a piece of my heart with her."

One of the cats on the table yawns, stretches, then jumps into my mother's lap, startling her slightly. The cat nestles, curls up, and purrs loudly. My mother runs a cupped hand over the cat's stiff ears; the cat closes its eyes contentedly.

Mina straightens some of the piles of papers and pictures on the table. Her tears change the color of her eyes to a murky blue-gray that looks like the sea. Placing her wet hankie in her lap, she awkwardly reaches up her sleeve to the mountain range of lumps just below her elbow where she stores more hankies, more tissues. She pulls out a couple, lifts her glasses onto her forehead, and holds a tissue at the corners of her eyes.

"After you left, things quickly got worse," Mina continues. "The day you left, I helped you pack and went with you and your parents to the boat. Later that day, I was beaten up and had my clothes taken from me. The men who beat me kept yelling at me, '*Niemand tut etwas für die Juden.* No one is to do anything for the Jews.'"

"I . . . I didn't know," my mother says, her eyes widening with a pained expression. "I didn't know of all the things that happened to you." Propping her elbows on the table, she rests her forehead in both trembling hands.

"No, of course not," Mina says. "How could you?"

"You never wrote me those things after I left." The line between Mom's eyebrows creases deeply as she focuses on Mina, looking from one eye to the other, trying desperately to understand what happened.

"Why would I?" Mina asks, shrugging her shoulders. "I didn't want you to worry."

"It's just . . ." Mom continues with a penetrating look. "It's just that I thought a lot about my parents. I guess I never gave much thought to how your life would be in Germany . . . to how your life would be different because of your friendship with our family." Mom stops, considers that, and then elaborates, "I guess I thought . . . I thought, because you weren't Jewish, you were safe."

"No," Mina says with an ironic, angry snort. "It didn't work like that. I was always marked . . . marked by my friendship to your family. The troubles didn't stop when you left. That was only the beginning."

Now come the stories, one angry tale after another, about the endless creativity and mean-spiritedness with which the *Schweinehunde* tormented her and the Westerfeld family. There was the time someone put manure on the front stoop so anyone using the door would step in it. Another time, someone killed one of the family's cats and left its body inside the front door of the house.

Then there was the evening, just after my mother left, when my grandfather went to the local pub to have a glass of wine. While he sat at the bar, someone began to play the national anthem and the room rose. One woman insisted that he stand up. The men jeered and jostled him to try to make him comply, but Siegmund refused. He came home and said, "That's the last time I go there."

Mom repeatedly turns her head from side to side as if she could shake off the story Mina tells. Still, farmers continued to do business with my grandfather, Mina says, because he paid more for the pickles than anyone else in the area. "I remember Herr Westerfeld removed the doorbells," she says, "so customers could come without being noticed." But then Müller, who lived across the street, watched the house. He wrote down the names of Herr Westerfeld's customers and organized a boycott of the business. Soon after, someone covered the walls of the business with graffiti. Eventually, they stationed a guard in front of the business so no one would go in the shop.

By this time, Mina says, things had become very difficult for the Westerfelds. They had no business. No money. No food. At last, she says, Herr Westerfeld had to let her go.

"He wrote me a letter of recommendation." She stops to shuffle through the pile of papers. "I know it's in here somewhere." When she can't find it, she says, "It doesn't matter. I still have it memorized. It said, 'We are sorry to have to let Mina Lautenschläger go, but we can no longer afford to keep her. She is correct, honest, and hardworking. We were always very satisfied with her work.'

"My mother couldn't stand to see the family treated this way," Mina continues. "So, one day, she hid a huge pot of stew under her apron and went to the Westerfelds' and knocked on the door. This was very dangerous, since no one was to go near there. No one answered, so my mother put the pot inside the door."

Her mother, Mina says, had been cleaning house for Müller for thirty years. When Müller saw her put the pot in the door, he confronted her. She told him, "I washed your diapers. I helped raise you. I can tell you what I think. This cannot happen. *Du kannst das diesen Leuten nicht antun.* You cannot do this to people."

That day, after all those years with the Müller family, Mina's mother was fired.

Mina gets up, coughs, puts some water in an old teakettle, sets it on the stove, and turns on the burner. I watch her smack her thin lips together, massaging the top lip with the bottom. She looks disgusted, as if telling the stories has broken a dike, releasing all the emotions that flooded her decades ago.

One day, she says, she walked past the house and heard all kinds of moaning and yelling inside. Oma Sara, who was a big woman, had fallen in the house and she couldn't get up. Frau Westerfeld couldn't lift her. Mina went to Bürgermeister Müller and told him, "We must help." He said, "Don't go in there." She ignored him and sneaked through three backyards so she could enter through a rear door.

"It was the only human thing to do," she explains, standing near the stove. "Then I helped lift Oma Sara onto the bed and Frau Westerfeld said, 'God must have sent you.'"

God? I'm taken aback. Astonished, really. After all she had lived through—the torment, the persecution, the humiliation—my grandmother still believed in God? I'd like to ask my mother, but I don't want to sidetrack Mina or disengage my mother from the conversation.

"Ahhh, Tiddy," Mina says. The chair scrapes the floor as she sits down again. "It got so ugly, so bad. You wouldn't have believed it, and it got harder and harder to stay away from it. Everywhere you went, you were forced to support the Nazis.

"I remember I was trying to get a job as a housekeeper so I took a cooking class twice a week to learn recipes and skills. In the class, everyone was to get up and sing and put up the flag for the Nazis. They sang the SA march—you know, the one that's about long life for Adolf Hitler. It was everywhere at the time, and whenever they sang it, everyone stood up. But I refused to do either.

"The teacher came over to me after class and said, 'You better do this. When you are living under the wolves, you have to howl.' But when I came home that night, I promised myself and I wrote it down here."

She points to some handwriting in black ink scrawled on the back of a picture of Frieda. Near the date—September 16, 1938—Mina wrote in German, "*Ich will niemals mit den Wolfen heulen. I will never howl with those wolves.*"

Mina refused to stand for the Nazi national anthem. She wouldn't put a Heil Hitler sign in her window. She wouldn't salute Hitler. "But I paid for it," she says, shaking her head. "In a way, I paid all my life."

I think of Hans's discomfort and Mina's fire. Maybe she was the town's only voice of opposition, resistance, and conscience. Certainly, then and now, she lived according to her own sense of morality. For it, the community ostracized her. No one knows where she lives, no one wants to know her, no one wants to be reminded of her. She is an untouchable, shunned like the Jewish cemetery.

For many in Stockstadt, she was easy to write off: Mina aligned herself with the Jews, and therefore she was a kind of Jew, too, guilty by association. Worse, she insisted on raising basic moral questions. By not howling with the wolves, she challenged everyone who did.

"What made you so different?" I ask her, as the teakettle begins to whistle. She gets up, shuts off the burner, but doesn't pour tea or coffee. Instead, she returns to her chair.

"First, the Jews in town were my friends," she says, gesturing to my mother. "After your family was no longer there for me, I was alone.

"But, really, my love for your family was only part of it. I just felt you can't do this to people."

"But why . . . ?" I persist. "Why were you so different from the rest? Were you religious?"

"No, not really," she says. "I mean, I was brought up in the church every Sunday and I prayed. But we weren't a deeply religious family. Still, we believed there were certain Christian rules. God would not allow this. You cannot behave like this to another man. You just can't."

I'm frustrated. Mina hasn't really given me a good answer. Maybe there isn't one. Maybe she was different, and that's all that can be said. If only a few others thought like Mina, maybe none of this would have happened. I wonder about the people we met yesterday, then urge my mother to tell Mina about the reunion.

"You know," Mom says in German, "yesterday we saw many people from the town at a reunion my class held in my honor."

"A reunion?" Mina asks skeptically, as if she can't understand why my mother would go; she can't even grasp the concept. "What kind of reunion?"

"For my grammar-school class."

"Who did you see?" Mina asks.

"Karl Schumacher, Ingrid Kraft, Louis Goldenburgher," my mother says. With each name, Mina breathes more and more heavily; the weight presses harder and she begins to cough. ". . . Ehrich, and Hahn." At the last name, she is clutching her chest, hacking, and reaching again for the inhaler.

"*Ach*," she says as she sprays, "be careful, Tiddy. You should not go near those people." She barely gets her words out and tries to sputter something between coughs.

When, finally, her asthma loosens its grip, she adds, "Those at the reunion, their parents were Nazis and they haven't changed. I'm sure of it," she says adamantly. "I'm absolutely sure of it. I would pull my house to the end of the earth to prove that to you."

Rifling through an envelope and pulling out a yellowed scrap of paper with a list of names on it, she says, "Look here. In 1940, I wrote down the names of the worst Nazis in Stockstadt. Some of the families of those at the reunion are on the list."

She points to the names, one after another, some that even I recognize. "Your classmates don't want to remember, Tiddy, and they don't want you to know, but their parents were all a part of it." Several coughs punctuate her statement; the past is choking her.

"Mina, please," my mother says. She stands up and walks over to the window that the outdoor shutters seal.

"I will never make peace with them and I will never forget what those families did."

"Mina, please," Mom says again, cutting her hand through the air and then slapping it on her thigh. "That was 1940. It was a long time ago."

"Not to me," Mina gasps immediately. "*Ich kann das nicht vergeben*. I cannot forgive them. They howled with the wolves."

"But, Mina," Mom argues, as she sits in her chair again and pulls it closer to the table. "You're talking about things that happened more than fifty years ago." Then she adds for emphasis, "Fifty years ago. *Fünf-zig Jahre her*."

"If you were here," Mina says—the fire in her eyes looks as if it has been stoked—"and saw what they did, you would be less forgiving."

"You've got to put the past in the past," my mother counters, asserting the slogan she has selected for her own life. Easier said than done, I think; so many times I've heard her say it, yet only occasionally seen any sign that she could do it. "It's behind you now."

"Not to me," Mina says, shaking her head emphatically and raising her voice. "Not after all the things they did to your family and all the things they did to me. They were always following and taunting me because I defended the Jews. They said that I was a prostitute for the Jews. One day, a package came in the mail for me. Over the address someone had written, 'He who eats with the Jews will die.'"

The stories gush forth; talking faster and louder, Mina builds her case, recalling each injustice etched in her memory, every story permanently stored on her mind's hard drive.

"Once Müller spit on my shoes because he said I was a friend of the Jews. He made me pay twenty marks because a town citizen charged that my new bike light didn't work. Of course, it did work. Twenty marks was a lot of money for me at the time.

"I could go on and on," she says, catching her breath and gesturing with both hands. "All this went on for years. They wouldn't even let me get married when I wanted to. The Bürgermeister refused to sign the necessary papers. So you see why I never forgive them, why I never forget."

My mother is trying to interrupt, to squeeze a word in, but Mina's story will not be delayed. In 1941, she continues, she applied for a caregiver's job at Phillipps Hospital, between Stockstadt and Crumstadt. She didn't get the job because the Bürgermeister Müller told the staff that Mina was "politically undesirable." After that, she realized that there was nothing left for her in Stockstadt. She had to leave, for she had been cast out by the town of her birth.

So she went from city to city looking for work: Darmstadt, Frankfurt, Berlin. No one would hire her because Müller had put out the word. Finally, she got a housekeeping job with a family in Berlin, but it didn't last; once the family learned that she had tried to help the Jews, they fired her. Then she worked for another family, who didn't belong to the Nazi Party. But when she learned that they supported the Nazis, she quit.

Eventually, she found work in the home of a man who held a high position with a Berlin bank. But he opposed the financing of the Holocaust, and it wasn't long before he lost his job. The banker belonged to a group of freethinkers, Mina says. The Nazis tried to find out who they were, in order to control or stop them. There was only one movement, and that was Nazism; all others were forbidden. In 1942, the banker decided to take his family to Poland, where all the conscientious objectors went. Mina, feeling unwelcome in her homeland, wanted to go along.

Just before leaving for Poland, Mina says, she decided to get married. But in order to marry, she had to document her family tree dating back to the 1870s to prove that she was Aryan. She needed letters of recommendation and character testimony signed and sworn by people who knew her.

"The only people I could turn to," she says, "were your sister, Betty, and the head of the other Jewish family, Moses Kahn. They sent me the letters from America." My mother nods as if she knew something about this. Only then did they sign the papers so Mina could marry. Her husband went with her to Poland.

Day and night, meetings were held in the family's new home, she recalls. People would come from the front and tell what was really happening. Here, she learned how the Germans were behaving in Russia, burning villages and killing civilians.

"While there," she says, finally breathing freely, "I became pregnant with my son, Jürgen. The government provided things for pregnant women, and gave me permission to go to this warehouse and get some clothes for the baby and for myself.

"I didn't realize until I got there that it was set up at a concentration camp," she says in a near-whisper. "When I went in the building, I realized what this was."

Her eyes are wide now, as if she's seeing it all for the first time, as she says in a low voice, "There were women's things—maternity dresses, shoes, purses, and stockings, even lipstick and hairpins." She pulls an old-fashioned pin out of her hair to make her point. "There were baby clothes—booties, diapers, bonnets, and little hand-knitted sweaters."

She holds her hands inches apart to show how small the clothes were. "There were even baby cups and rattles," she says, her tone dropping still further. "These were the belongings of Jewish mothers and babies who had been killed." Now her voice cracks.

"I wouldn't take anything," she sneers, slicing the air with her hand and slamming it on the table in fury. The cats jump and spike out the hairs on their backs like porcupine quills. One lets out an angry hiss, but Mina doesn't notice.

"This was so terrifying to me," she says with a shudder, "I couldn't sleep for weeks." Now she pauses, making a sour face. "*Sie machen mich krank*. They make me sick," she spits again. "*Schweinehunde*. It made me crazy." Her cough has gripped her again, and we wait, helpless, as she works to bring her breathing under control.

"Yet, I felt I had to survive, especially once my marriage ended and I had my young son," Mina resumes. "I saw what was happening around me, but I couldn't say anything, because if I did they'd kill me or put me in camp. A lot of people vanished back then."

Eventually, Mina returned to Germany, but was labeled a displaced person. "When I finally came back to Stockstadt, I started seeing again a man I had known years earlier named Paul, a German officer who became an American POW." She takes out a black-and-white photograph of a handsome young man in a German soldier's uniform and shows it to us. "This is what Paul looked like in 1933," she says with pride. Then she explains that she had been in love with Paul since 1936, long before she married her first husband. But she was not allowed to marry him then, because he was in the army and she was a friend of a Jewish family.

Watching her look dreamily at this long-ago picture of her young man is strange, almost incongruent. How is it that this Jew-by-association, this Aryan who refused to be a good German, could love a German soldier? I'm barely able to contain the question, but I don't want to be rude.

"He was so good-looking and well educated," she continues. "He spoke several languages and was good in writing and counting. He had a profession. He made me happy and he became a wonderful father to my son."

They married, she says, and lived for a while in Stockstadt. After the war, he worked at the U.S. Air Force base in Darmstadt. But Mina says she never felt comfortable living in Stockstadt. So, in the 1950s, they moved to Tromm. He died in 1981.

Finally, there is a pause. Mom seems to want to speak. She inhales as if she were about to begin a sentence and then, instead of words, releases a long exhale. "After . . . After I left," she stumbles, "did you . . . did you keep up with the family?" She asks so tentatively that I wonder whether she truly wants an answer.

"Yes," Mina says. "Of course I did."

"I always wondered what happened to . . . to Uncle Ludwig, the one with the car?" my mother asks. He is a safe subject—a family member known to all, but not an immediate relative. "I know he lived a long time in concentration camp, but I never heard if he survived."

"He was a real fighter," Mina recalls with the hint of a smile. "He would always say, 'I'll make it through this.' But he couldn't hang on long enough. Four weeks before the war ended, I heard that he died."

"Do you know . . ." Mom hesitates again, debating whether to finish her question, then gathers her courage. "Do you know what happened to my . . . my parents?"

"Well, they were forced to sell the house, and the proceeds were deposited in a blocked account," Mina says. "For a while, they were allowed to rent one room from Frey"—Günter's father. "Frey was not nice. He gave them two rooms that had no common entrance. One had no heat, and the other was the smallest in the house. They had to put some stuff in storage. Your teacher, the one who tried to make your father send you to school on Saturdays, bought the other house, the one belonging to your cousins, the other Jewish family.

"By this time, your parents realized that they had to get out, but they got some bad advice about how to proceed from a cousin of yours. Worse, the passport office was crooked. The police presidium, where the passport office was located, issued numbers but didn't stick to them. They took bribes and let people who knew someone in the office go ahead of the others."

Mina closes her eyes, shakes her head in disbelief. "I remember your father saying that the system stank. It was very political. Had that not been the case, they could have been one of the first to leave. They had a very good number." Resting her elbows on the table and framing her face with her hands, Mom shakes her head in anguish, reflecting Mina's disgust.

Mina explains that all the Jews kept going to the passport office in Stuttgart, where officials maintained a constant state of chaos. They sent Jews seeking to leave Germany from office to office, to wait in line for hours and fill out dozens of forms. Meanwhile, the German officials would put off making decisions, forcing people to come back again and again. These delays were actually a conscious effort to get the Jews to trade all their money and goods for a passport.

"Finally, Oma Sara got a passport on September 9, 1940," Mina says, again amazing me with her memory for dates. "They granted one to her because she was old. When Oma returned home that night after picking up her passport in Stuttgart, she died."

"What . . . What did she die of?" my mother asks. "Had she been sick?"

"No, not really," Mina says. "She was always talking about how she didn't really want to leave Germany. She'd say she was afraid to go on the boat. She thought she would be thrown overboard and eaten by the sharks. We thought that maybe she died from fear."

Mina says that Frieda and Siegmund never did get passports, but they kept trying. They had no money and no way to make money, so they decided to move to Darmstadt. "There," Mina continues, "your father got a job for a while at your uncle's furniture store, where he had worked when he went to college. This would have been, let's see, February of 1941, when your parents lived at Sudetengaustrasse 50 in Darmstadt."

Soon after that, Mina says, my grandfather was taken to the camp at Sachsenhausen. "He lived a long time in the camps," she says.

"*Ja,*" my mother says, wiping her red nose with a tissue.

"He was there so long that your mother would go visit him once in a while. I remember one day Frau Westerfeld sent a package of bread to Herr Westerfeld, but then she didn't hear from him for four weeks. So she got permission to see him. They talked through the barbed-wire fence, and when she took his hand through the wire, she gave him a piece of salami hidden in her palm. An SS guard saw what she had done, and as she turned, he smacked her across the face."

My mother covers her eyes and tears drop from her cheeks. She picks up a tissue on the table, dabs her eyes, and then covers her open mouth with it.

"A few months later, Frau Westerfeld was forced to move into an apartment with a Jewish family named Isaac who had six kids." Mina explains that the Nazis had forced all the Jews in the area to live in one building, called a "Jew-house." The Nazis would go to these buildings and collect Jews to work for very low pay.

"Every time I visited your mother in Darmstadt, I had to flirt or lie to the Nazi police who guarded the building. Frau Westerfeld never wanted anyone to come, because she feared for their lives. She'd say to me, 'Please, Mina, don't come. Things are bad enough for us. Don't endanger your life.' But I ignored her."

A muffled "*danke*" comes from behind the tissue covering my mother's mouth.

"Anyway," Mina continues in a slow sad tone, "in the winter of 1942, the police got all the names of the Jews who lived in your mother's building by promising food to the apartment manager if he provided a list of the occupants. He cooperated."

She swallows hard and wipes her eyes with her tissue, though she isn't crying now. The story isn't finished, but she doesn't know quite how to go on. She swallows again, looks away from my mother and me, and continues.

Now, oddly, Mina almost looks as if she feels guilty or responsible for what happened. My mother doesn't take her eyes off Mina.

"I came to visit her a couple of days later," she says, as if she were giving testimony. Her eyes are fixed on the window, though she cannot see out beyond the tightly closed shutters.

"The neighbors gave me the news." Her head drops onto her chest at the memory. "They said that at six in the morning on March 23, 1942, Isaac, his six children, and the other Jews living in the building"—Mina now speaks so softly that it's almost impossible to hear her—"including Frau Westerfeld, were taken to Camp Biaski in Lublin, Poland."

Mina rises, signifying that that is all she has to say, and gets out the matches to relight the burner under the teakettle. She stoops over the stove, the weight of the past pressing down on her frail body. A blue flame erupts under the teakettle and steam rises from the spout; the water is still hot.

My mother sits motionless, her eyes fixed on the spot where Mina sat. I wonder if she's noticed that Mina is no longer there. I rub my mother's forearm to try to comfort her. At first, she doesn't respond. But then she turns her gaze to me, wipes her eyes, and pats my hand, suggesting that she'll be okay.

"Tell me something," Mina says, when she returns to the table and sits down. "Do you know whether you're having a boy or a girl?" She takes my hand and rubs it. "I know they can do all these new tests now to figure out the sex of the baby."

"They can do them, and I actually had the test." I find my voice, immensely relieved to change the subject. "But I didn't find out the baby's sex. I wanted it to be a surprise."

"You have children at home, yes?"

"Yes, two sons."

"So I'm sure you're hoping for a girl."

"Well, yes," I say, "I am. But . . . But, as my mother always says, 'We'll love whatever we get.'" My mother looks at me, eyes brightening. She's pleased that I've quoted her and lets me know with a slight, loving smile.

"I always wanted to have another child," Mina says, looking off dreamily, "and I had hoped it would be a girl. I had a name all picked out for my daughter." She turns and looks directly at my mother, tears welling in her eyes. "I wanted to call her Edith."

My mother places her hand on top of Mina's and mine and we sit together in silence. To me, Mina and my mother seem like sisters. It's not any physical resemblance; they look not at all alike, this gray-blond Aryan and this dark Jew. But in their movements, in their strikingly similar mannerisms, they mirror each other. Even more striking, they have the easy comfort of sisters whose foundation is shared history.

After a while, Mina gets up and this time leaves the room without saying a word. When she returns, she is carrying a brown grocery bag. "I have a few things for you," she says, as if she had anticipated our visit.

Reaching in the bag, she takes out a ring case and hands it to me. "My husband Paul gave this to me as an engagement gift. I doubt I'll have a daughter-in-law; I don't think my Jürgen will ever get married, now that he's close to fifty. I doubt I'll have a granddaughter."

I spring open the old velvety, aqua-blue ring box, unveiling a large glimmering square-cut emerald in a simple rose-gold setting. I don't know what to say, or whether I should accept such a precious, personal gift.

"It's beautiful," I tell Mina through my mother, "but I don't think I should accept this." I close the box and try to hand it back to her.

"But you must," Mina insists, pushing my hand away. "I want you to have it. To me, you are the closest thing to a daughter that I will ever know."

"Take it," my mother says, supporting Mina. I reach for my purse and tuck the box into its safest spot, an inside zipper pocket.

"I also want you to have these papers." She gathers up the yellow envelopes that contain her notes, letters, and pictures, including the one of my grandmother on which Mina vowed never to howl with the wolves. "They belong in your family," she adds as she hands them to me.

"And I have something else for you." She reaches deeper into the paper bag. "The last time I saw your grandmother, she was unwrapping the tea set Tiddy, Betty, and I played with as children. You remember them"— Mina turns to my mother—"the china set with blue-and-gold trim that your wealthy relatives from Cologne sent us around Christmas one year. We begged Frau Westerfeld to let us play with them. For a long time, she said, 'No. They are too fancy and too fragile to use as toys.'

"But when it became clear that she would have to send you and Betty to America, she gave them to us. In our last months together—especially after Betty left—we played with them all the time. Remember, Tiddy? We would always set a place for Betty."

Mina reaches into the paper bag, pulls out a wad of newspaper, and carefully unrolls it, revealing a small china cream pitcher in a yellowed white finish, its royal-blue border trimmed with faded, hand-painted gold flowers. She places the creamer on the table, pulls out another ball of newspaper, and unwraps a teapot from the same child-size set. My mother picks up the creamer, fingering this archeological treasure that I suspect she barely remembers. The paper rattles loudly as Mina unveils a cracked sugar bowl, three cups, and their saucers. She arranges them neatly in a half-circle, as if she were setting the table for a tea party.

"The last time I saw Frau Westerfeld," Mina continues, "she was thinking she must sell the tea set to get some money to buy food. But instead she looked at me, held up the teapot, and said, '*Willst du sie haben*? Maybe you would like these?'"

Mina carefully places its chipped lid on the tiny teapot and turns to me. "*Willst du sie haben*? Maybe *you* would like these?" she asks gently.

The bare bulb hanging over the table casts long, dark shadows behind the fragile, miniature tea set. Mina carefully picks up a tiny cup and, with unspeakable tenderness, places it in both of my hands.

"I'm hoping you will have a daughter," Mina says, as she folds my fingers around the cup, "and you'll pass the tea set along to her."

She closes her eyes for a long moment. I suppose the three of us are picturing a dark-haired, dark-eyed little girl in a quiet room, singing and talking to herself as she pours tea.

When Mina opens her eyes, she adds, "Be sure to tell her that the tea set is an heirloom. Tell her it comes from her great-grandmother."

Chapter 11

We are lying in bed, my mother and I, in the Stockstadt hotel after a long, tiring Saturday of sightseeing: a castle, rock formations, a petting zoo, and a museum. This morning, when my mother called Hans to ask him to join us, he declined. My mother thanked him for taking so much time with us and for everything he had done this week. They exchanged warm goodbyes, promising to stay in touch.

So we were on our own today, following tourist maps and directions at information booths to take in a few sights before leaving tomorrow.

Now the darkness blanketing our bed creates an odd trust between us, a faceless feeling that confers a sense of security, like the curtain separating priest from sinner in the old-fashioned confessional booth. Relieved of the daunting necessity of looking at each other, we are free to open delicate topics or old wounds, to say things we would normally avoid. The dark gives our quiet talk the detached, safe feeling of a telephone conversation.

"You know," my mother's voice cracks, "I slept in my mother's bed the night before I left Germany."

Lying on my back, I peer into the darkness and realize I'm seeing those strange, colorful flashes and dots that fill a child's night vision—the flickering personal fireworks that rarely visit adults. I watch but don't speak, because I don't know what to say.

Is she finally going to tell me of the private, painful moments before she left? It was her pivotal event, and mine, the moment in which I was made long before I was born, the experience I never had but couldn't escape. It is the scene she kept these many years in that mental safe-deposit box of hers. I always knew it was there—it had to be—but I thought she had lost the key, or maybe thrown it out.

"My mother never let me in her bed, even when I had a nightmare," she continues, in a voice so soft that it's almost a whisper. If I didn't know she was speaking, I wouldn't recognize her. "But that night, she asked me to sleep with her."

"Oh?" I say, to encourage her to continue.

"I remember, just before going to bed, we were sitting near the old wood-burning stove in the living room when she said, 'I feel so cold. I want you near me.'"

"So what did you do?" I ask.

"I took the only stuffed toy I had, a boy doll I called 'Arno'—I slept with him every night—and crawled into bed with her."

She stops, and I wonder whether she intends to go on. Then, as if her memory is speaking, she says slowly, "I curled close to her with my face next to hers. She was shivering. She didn't try to explain things or give me any advice. We didn't really talk.

"The only thing she said was she loved me—I don't know that she ever told me that before. She never said what she felt. She didn't show it, either. But that night, she stroked my hair with her hand until I fell asleep.

"The next day, we rushed around to catch an early train in Stockstadt that would take me to the dock in Hamburg. Mina came with us—you remember, she told us that. I was the second child my parents had to see off; my sister had left a year earlier.

"I sat next to the window in the train, watching my whole world pass by. The church, the graveyard, the Town Hall, our house. I remember looking out the train window and wondering whether the storks would return to the bell tower if I wasn't there to wait for them."

"Did you talk on the train?" I ask, realizing that this is probably my only chance to know.

"Not really. I don't think any of us said too much. I guess no one knew what to say. We tried to act like . . . we'd see each other soon. Like this was only a short separation."

"Did you believe that?"

"Well, I wanted to believe it. We pretended that this wasn't forever. But . . . but I suppose, somehow, I knew it was." She stops and shifts on the bed.

"When we got to the boat, my parents worried about my ticket, my passport, and my bag. Both of my parents asked me several times about those things. They hung my ticket and my passport on a string around my neck, tucked between my coat and my dress." She stops and then remembers, "They were concerned because I always was losing things. Even Mina made me pull out my passport to prove I still had it."

"So," I say, trying to pull her back to her story, "were there lots of children at the boat?"

"Yes, some were there by themselves. We were getting on a smaller boat that would take us to the *Deutschland*. Some children were crying and screaming. Others, the older ones, just looked worried."

"What about you?" I ask. "Were you worried?"

"I was, but I was trying not to show it. And I didn't really understand what was happening."

"And your parents?" I press. "How did they seem?"

"At the dock, my mother didn't say much. She fussed over a button on my coat. The top hole was loose, so she kept buttoning it for me. Once when she fixed it, I noticed her hand was trembling.

"I kissed and hugged my father. He told me, 'Don't worry, Tiddy. We'll be together again soon.' And then I hugged Mina, who cried and made me promise to write every week. But my mother wouldn't look me in the eye or say anything."

"So what did she do?"

"She kissed me on the forehead, turned me by the shoulders, and directed me to the metal bridge to board the ship. I clutched Arno as I slowly walked onto the bridge . . . alone."

"Did you go onto the deck so that you could wave goodbye?" I ask, trying to keep her from withdrawing and becoming buried in her own thoughts.

"Yes. It took a long time for the ship to leave the dock. So I stood watching and waving to my parents. They waited and waited, never taking their eyes off me. I felt uncomfortable and kind of wished that the ship would just leave.

"But then, when the ship finally pulled away from the harbor, I saw some of the parents collapse on the ground. My parents stood frozen, just the way they look in pictures. As the blue between us grew wider, I watched them get smaller, and I realized my life had changed forever.

"A kind of sadness I had never felt before came over me. It wasn't the way you feel as a child. It was more of the heaviness an adult feels when someone dies. I realized that nothing would ever be the same. My childhood was over.

"I opened my mouth to scream. Somehow, I thought if I screamed maybe everything would stop—the ship, the blue, even Hitler. I opened my mouth . . . but I . . . I couldn't make a sound. I fell to my knees on the deck and clung to my parents with my eyes. I watched them become dots. Then they completely disappeared in the distance."

She swallows and adds in a hoarse voice, "Then all I could see was the blue."

She stops speaking, takes a deep breath, and brings her knees up under the covers. The silence is a relief. She clears her throat to continue—but her tone has shifted abruptly.

"I've never been able to understand it," she steams, suddenly incensed. "How could they do it?"

"What?" I ask, confused.

"How could they send me away?"

"But they didn't just send you away," I say incredulously. I run her question through my mind; what can she be thinking? "Imagine how desperate your mother must have been to reach that decision."

"But how . . . how could she stand there and watch me go?"

"Just imagine how hard it was for her," I say, baffled that we are even having this conversation. "Imagine what it felt like for her to see that ship leave the dock."

My heart tears as I picture my grandmother, any mother, standing on that dock. "She was there because she didn't see any other option," I try to explain. "Your parents didn't believe that they could get out of Germany. So they had no choice."

"No, that's not true," she argues. "Of course they had a choice. They could have chosen to let me stay with them."

"What?" I say, struck by her irrationality. I have an impulse to throw on the lights, as if that would make her see things more clearly.

Instead, I contain myself and press on, "But you would have died."

"Yes," she sighs, as if that wouldn't have mattered much. "But at least I would have been with them. We would have been together."

"Mom," I say, "I know it seems cruel, but she did what any loving parent would do. She did what was best for you."

"You don't understand. It was so hard to live without them." I hear her pull a few tissues from a box on the floor next to the bed. "It was so cruel."

"But, Mom . . ." I prop myself up on an elbow and face her, though I can't see her. "Nothing could be more loving than sending you away so that you could live."

"But all I really wanted," she sputters through tears, "all I wanted was to stay with them."

"Mom, parents do what's best for their children, even when it hurts them. It's instinct to save your child."

I don't know that I'm getting through to her. Neither of us says anything for a few minutes. This seems so crazy, yet so important for her to understand.

So I try a new approach to build my case. "You know," I say, "I just finished reading a novel where a family is on vacation and a toddler gets bitten by a spider—it's a black widow, I think—and has an allergic reaction. The child's airways swell up and she can't breathe. They call the nearest doctor, who is at a hospital forty miles away. He tells the father that he must rush the girl to the hospital, but if the girl's throat closes on the way, the father will have to perform a tracheotomy in the car. The doctor tells the father how to cut his daughter's throat and windpipe without causing her to bleed to death.

"So the mother drives and the father sits in the back seat with the girl on his lap. The dad sings songs like 'I've got sixpence, jolly, jolly sixpence,' to his daughter to keep her quiet. Under his sleeve, he hides his Swiss Army knife, at the ready, in case he has to cut her throat to save her life.

"In a way, that's what your parents did for you—hurt you to save your life. It's probably the most selfless thing any parent can do and, in many ways, it hurts them more than it hurts you."

"No, I don't think so," she argues. "Maybe what they did was selfish. By sending me away, they took a stand against Hitler, and maybe, to them, that was the most important thing. They wanted me to live. They wanted the family to go on."

"Like you were a remaining genetic specimen, to ensure that the family carried on?" I say skeptically. "I don't think so."

"But"—she breaks down, her voice sounding muffled as she gasps into her tissue—"they didn't really think about me, about what happened to me. They didn't think about what it would be like to go on without them."

What she cannot see, will never see, is an image that floats into my expectant-mother mind: In a way, her parents gave birth twice to the same child. First they gave her life, and then they did it again by saving her from Hitler. But when her parents sent her away, my mother was a child—too young to comprehend the necessity, too old to overcome the loss.

If my mother had been a survivor, maybe she would be grateful, and could have felt each day as a gift, every year as a mission. But as an escapee, she feels she doesn't deserve to live. For that matter, she's not sure she wants to . . . not without her parents.

Her understanding is stuck in a twelve-year-old's broken heart. All she can know is that her mother and her Motherland abandoned and rejected her, and that's what she can never escape.

Maybe, I think, I should try a different strategy. Maybe if I can get her to put herself in her parents' place I can make her see that theirs was an act of love. "Mom, don't . . . don't you think . . ." I stop and wonder whether I really want to ask her this question; she might answer me, and any answer she gives me will hurt.

"Mom, don't you think you would have tried to save me?" My voice quivers; I seem to be asking the question of the darkness.

She says nothing. I wish I could see her face so that I would know how to read her silence. "I . . . I don't," she finally mumbles. "I don't think I could do it. I couldn't have stood on that dock. I . . . I just couldn't live without you."

Then she revises her answer and her tone: "Don't ask me that," she says in her snappish, annoyed-mother voice. "I don't know . . . I don't know that I can answer it."

The conversation is over. Mom ends it by turning her back to me, as if she's going to sleep. She doesn't even say good night.

I turn away from her.

Darkness still surrounds me when I open my eyes in the early morning. Nothing is familiar, and for a moment I panic, wondering where I am. Then I realize that a body is spooned around me—not my husband's; this is a different fit. A hand knobby and veined, hangs over my shoulder, a heavy weight of need. I am tucked into the arc of my mother's body. The rhythmic breathing of her sleep blows past my ear. The baby snailed within me shifts. I don't move. The three of us are a Venn diagram of maternity; an invisible fourth circle is overlaid upon us.

I hear the words my mother uttered just before we went to sleep; they stab my heart. *It was so hard to live without them.* Now I see that neither my mother nor her mother should be resented for how she coped with what happened to her. With love and confusion, they both, like every mother, tried to spare their children their own fate.

Still, what parents do echoes in a child's life. *It was so cruel . . . How could they send me away?*

And because she couldn't accept that they sent her away, she could never send me away. Not without reliving her own loss. Not without feeling that by growing up, living independently, building my own life, I had severed the most basic bond of our relationship. It was a kind of betrayal.

When she and my father drove me to college in the late summer of 1972, the car ride took on a doomed, claustrophobic mood as she stared out the window, never saying a word, her tears, sighs, and quiet gasps punctuating the silence. Surely, in any parent's life, joy and sadness fill these moments when a child begins to establish an independent life. But for my mother, this parting was much more than that; it was a funeral procession, a break like the one years earlier, when her parents took her to the boat.

The boat she could never get off.

Chapter 12

Six A.M., Sunday, time to load our baggage and drive to the airport. In a couple of hours we'll be on the plane, heading for home. At this hour it's still dark, though the sky is streaked with the pink, orange, and lavender hues of sunrise.

The last bag is stashed in the Rabbit and I go around to the driver's side. Just as I'm about to open the door, my mother calls from the other side of the car, "Wait a minute!"

"What's the matter?" I ask, thinking we've left something up in the room.

"I want to drive," she says.

This catches my attention. "You . . . you want to drive?" I ask skeptically.

"Yes."

Mom has never once taken the wheel during our trip, never seemed comfortable even as a passenger in this German-made car. For most of the week, she sat stiffly, taking up as little space as possible in her seat, knees pushed together, elbows close to her body, and hands in her lap holding the maps.

"You're probably tired," she says, making a case. "We didn't get a lot of sleep last night." That's true, though it didn't seem to matter on any other morning during our stay.

"Besides," she adds, "I don't think I've ever driven one of these before." I know she hasn't. "You're sure?" I ask again.

"Yes, I'm sure," she says, coming around to the passenger side with her hand out for the keys. "I'll drive."

At the airport, we sit in a lobby awaiting our turn to check our luggage at the international terminal. I am digging through my purse, tossing out charge-card receipts, my old plane ticket, and the contract from the car rental. My mother has picked up her book again; she's still on page 109, right where she left off a week ago at O'Hare.

Glancing up for a moment, I notice a man slowly hobbling toward us with a familiar limp. I watch him dip from side to side, one arm loosely swinging in the same pattern, so that he keeps his balance. As he approaches us, he smiles broadly.

It's Karl Schumacher, the man injured in the war whom we talked to at the reunion. I nudge my mother; she looks up.

"Karl," my mother says, her voice radiating warmth. She gets up to shake his hand; he begins to talk, hanging on to her hand as he speaks.

"*Ich bin sehr froh, dass ich dich gefunden habe.* I'm so glad I found you," he says, puffing from the long walk to the lobby. "I was worried I'd have to walk all the way down the corridor, to the other baggage area." He stops for a moment, winded as if he had run a mile, and then adds, "Just to get this far, I had to stop every few minutes and catch my breath."

"What are you doing here at seven in the morning?" my mother asks.

"I had to come," he tells her, still out of breath. "I wanted to be here . . . to say goodbye to you."

They talk in German for a few minutes, exchanging addresses. But before they've had much time to visit, we're called up to the baggage counter.

Karl stands with us as we check in. A few minutes later, the flight attendant announces over the intercom in German and English that we are to board our plane.

"Thank you for coming, Karl," my mother says, throwing her arms around him in an enthusiastic embrace. Not expecting the hug, Karl stumbles slightly on his bad leg, gasping as he tries to save himself and my mother from tumbling to the floor. He manages to stay upright; so does she; and when they've found their footing, Karl's face turns bright red and they begin to laugh with the silliness of children.

I realize that I've never heard my mother laugh like this; it's an uncontrolled, high-pitched belly laugh emanating from deep within her. She slips a finger underneath her glasses to wipe a tear. Even after she and Karl have regained their composure, they burst into a spasm of giggles again.

Finally, Karl takes her hand and tells my mother what a pleasure it was to see her again: "*Es ist schön mit euch gewesen.*" As he turns toward me and we shake hands, he adds a few words about her *Tochter*. I assume he's telling her he's glad he got to meet me, too.

When we step into the corridor that leads to the gate, my mother turns around to wave to Karl.

"*Auf Wiedersehen,*" he calls to her, from the same spot where they stumbled.

"*Auf Wiedersehen,*" she echoes, with a certain closure in her voice.

"*Komm bald wieder zurück.* Come back again," he adds.

My mother smiles at Karl, her appreciative gaze lingering on his face. Then she breaks away, turning to walk slowly down the corridor toward the plane, clutching her passport and her ticket home.

We take our seats in the back section of the plane. "Did Karl come to the airport this morning just to say goodbye?" I ask my mother.

"Yes, I think so," she says.

"That's awfully early to get to the airport," I say, "especially when you don't have to be here."

"I think he felt he *did* have to be here," Mom replies. "He said he just couldn't let me go this time without seeing me off . . . without wishing me well." She looks at me intensely, her brown eyes dewy. Then she adds, "He couldn't let me go this time without saying goodbye."

After takeoff, we both doze. When I awaken, I look out the window at a gray sea of clouds and feel completely detached from the world below, or, for that matter, any world; it is that odd, disassociated sensation unique to flying that offers a rare perspective on life below.

I look over to my mother to see if she's still asleep. Leaning on an elbow and supporting her face with her thumb and index finger, she looks wide awake and full of thought. Her book rests in her lap, still open to page 109.

"We didn't get to see the old movie theater where I used to go just before I left," she says, letting me aboard her train of thought. "I wonder if it's still there."

"A theater in town?" I ask, surprised that a small town like Stockstadt had one.

"Yes," she says. "There was a theater not far from my house. Sunday afternoons, everyone in town went there. Back then, it cost ten pfennige to get in. Let's see, that would be less than a dime now. Can you imagine?"

"No, not really," I reply ruefully, thinking about the $7.50 we recently dropped for each ticket to see *Howards End.*

"About a year before I left," she says, pushing the arm rest that separated us into the back of the seat, "they told me that I couldn't go to the Sunday shows anymore. By this time, Betty and our Jewish cousins who had lived in town were gone. No one was to have anything to do with me."

"So did you quit going?"

"No," she says, shaking her head. I see by her glazed eyes that she is back in time. "I begged the theater owner to let me come in after the show had started so that no one would see that I was there, and I promised to leave early through a side exit. I really don't remember how

I convinced him." She stops to search her memory. "I think the owner felt sorry for me, since I was the only kid who wasn't allowed in the show. I remember all week I'd look forward to seeing the movie. It was a double thrill because, in some small way, I had gotten around the Nazis and I got to see some of the greats, like Emil Jannings and Greta Garbo."

"Did anyone ever catch you there?" I ask, picturing her as a little girl darting down the aisles, squeezing between the seats, and then skulking out of the darkened theater.

"No, I don't think so," she says, and then adds, placing her hand on her chest, "but my heart pounded, especially as I took a seat in the back row. I remember thinking that my heart was pounding so loud someone was sure to hear it. But no one ever knew I was there."

"Maybe someone saw you," I say, "but never told on you."

"I doubt it," she says. "If they had seen me, I'm sure they would have made a big deal of it.

"I must have snuck into that theater every week for a year," she says with a certain pride, and then adds, "until I left for America."

"I just can't imagine how scary coming to America must have been," I say. I had wanted to ask her about this for years. I know as little about her early life in Chicago as I knew about her life in Germany before we took this trip.

"I mean, you were only twelve and all by yourself," I add hopefully, pushing just a bit.

"Well, of course, other children came on the boat," Mom begins. "The Jewish Children's Bureau organized the trip and sponsored us. When we arrived in New York, they had arranged for a tour of the city—you know, the Statue of Liberty, the Empire State Building, and Radio City Music Hall."

I imagine her culture shock, going from the sleepy town of Stockstadt to bustling New York City, with cars thronging the streets and screeching by, towering skyscrapers above, and crowded sidewalks all around.

"That's what I remember most," she recalls, wide-eyed. "Radio City Music Hall. The Disney cartoon version of *Snow White and the Seven Dwarfs* had just been released and we saw it there.

"That," she adds with a tone of sureness, "was probably the scariest moment of all for me."

"Scariest?" After a year of sneaking into the Stockstadt theater, why would she be so frightened by an animated movie based on a fairy tale at an American theater in which she was welcome?

"Well," Mom answers, "do you remember the movie?"

"A little, I think," I say, trying to sort quickly through all the Disney features mixed up in my mind. "Is that the one with the wicked queen asking, 'Mirror, mirror on the wall, who's the fairest of them all?'"

"Well, yes, but I didn't understand much English," she goes on. "All I could figure out was that some jealous, scary witch tries to get one of her men to kill Snow White. He can't bring himself to do it, so he tells her to run away and never come back to her home or the kingdom. Snow White runs off into the dark woods, where all the trees look like scary creatures and thousands of eyes follow her everywhere. I worried that maybe this would be me; this was my future. I had come from a terrible situation and now arrived in some place that could be just as bad, maybe worse."

"*Was* it worse?" I ask, having never really considered that.

"Well . . ." She pauses, taking her time in answering me. "I can't say that it was worse. I was safe here, but it was different."

"You went to live with your aunt and uncle, right?"

"Yes," Mom replies. "On the boat, some children had gotten very close. But after the few days in New York, everyone went in different directions." She flits her hand like a bird. She became friends with one girl who was off to Seattle to be adopted by a foster family, though both had wished that they could go to Chicago together. My mother says they still keep up; the friend sent her a New Year's card this year describing her grandchildren and their activities.

"I took the train to Chicago," she says, placing her hand near her neck, "where I went to live with my father's brother, Jack, his wife, and their daughter, who was a little older than me. They had a big apartment in a Jewish neighborhood on the South Side."

We're interrupted as the flight attendant brings us our breakfast trays. My mother thanks her in German. She wipes her hands with the wet towelette and then struggles to open the plastic wrapping that holds her napkin and utensils.

"When did Uncle Jack come to America?" I ask, too curious about staying with this chapter in Mom's life to bother with my food.

"Oh, I think he came in 1910," she says, shaking her orange juice and breaking the seal. "He came to work for an uncle who made umbrellas. Anyway, Uncle Jack was okay about having me live with them. I think he helped arrange for my trip. He picked me up at the train station."

She takes a sip of her drink. When she sets it back on her tray, she adds, "But my aunt wasn't there. I don't think she really wanted me. I suppose she felt she had to take me in."

She pushes her eggs around with a fork, then decides to sip her coffee instead of eating. Steam from the coffee rises and, for a moment, fogs her glasses.

"So my aunt figured she'd get something out of the deal," my mother continues, her tone barely covering her resentment. "Each day, she would make a list of chores that she expected me to do: wash the floor, do the dishes, make the beds, dust, vacuum, clean the toilets."

"It sounds like Cinderella's wicked stepmother," I say, certain I have the right fairy tale this time. "From Snow White to Cinderella."

"Yeah, I suppose so," my mother says with a snort. "During the summer, I wasn't allowed to go anywhere until the chores were done. They could take all day. On Thursdays, my aunt would go out for the day. I'd race through the chores in the morning so that I could catch the train to Comiskey Park and be there for the first pitch of the White Sox game."

She pauses, and then, struck with guilt for criticizing, she adds, "I suppose my aunt and uncle were good to me; I mean, they did take me in. But I always felt like a guest. I remember Aunt Mildred would put out a fruit bowl and count how many apples, oranges, and bananas she placed in it. If a piece was missing, she would get annoyed and ask me if I ate it.

"I never felt that their home was my home," she adds.

"What about school?" I ask. "Did you feel any more comfortable there? Were you able to make friends?"

"No, not really. When I first arrived in Chicago, I should have been in seventh grade. But I didn't know the language, so the school placed me in first grade. Here I was, twelve years old, almost as tall as I am now"— Mom holds up her hand to show how big she was—"and a student in a classroom of little grammar-school children. I remember feeling so embarrassed. The little children whispered when I came into the room. And, worse, I couldn't even fit into the chairs; the teacher had to give me the chair from her desk. Eventually, as I learned the language, they moved me up through the grades."

"Oh," I say, wondering whether anyone at the school ever considered her socialization, ever thought about how she would adjust. "So practically everyone in the school got to have you in their class."

"Yeah, each time I entered a new classroom, I went through the same thing all over again," Mom answers. "Finally, just before I went to high school, I guess it would be the end of eighth grade, they put me in with the right classmates. But by this time, making friends wasn't easy."

Of course, she says, the students of her age teased her about being a first-grader. She asked too many questions. So many things puzzled her since she was unaccustomed to American ways. Her questions put off some girls who might have been her friends.

"Even in high school," she continues, "I didn't do too well with friends. Part of the problem was that I would have had to invite them over to my aunt's house, and she didn't really want that. So I never made much effort. That way, I wouldn't have to say to a friend, 'You can't come over.'"

She gazes at the pewter-gray light coming through the window of the airplane, and doesn't say anything for a moment.

"Every night for years," she goes on, her voice sounding softer, sadder now, "I would get into bed and, in my mind, I'd walk through my parents' house in Germany. I'd go from room to room, running my fingers along the furniture, picturing where the pots and the cooking utensils were kept in the kitchen, trying to remember the colors of a painting that hung in the living room or the titles of the books on the shelves. I'd try to hold on to my parents and my past by remembering

everything. When I couldn't remember something, I would get pan-
icky."

"But then, during my first year of high school, Mina sent me a letter
saying that the Nazis had killed both of my parents. That changed everything. I wouldn't let myself think about them anymore. I wouldn't allow
myself to get into bed and go into my parents' home again. Each time I'd
think of it, I'd block it out. It was like I'd closed the front door to the
house.

"I remember . . ." She looks away from me for a moment. Maybe
she's about to cry. "When I got the letter and read it, I began to cry." She
bites her bottom lip. "Aunt Mildred, who was never very loving, saw me
crying. Instead of comforting me or even just saying she was sorry, she
turned to me"—my mother pauses, licks her lips—"and said, 'What did
you expect?'"

I can say nothing; in this moment, words seem inadequate. She
seems to understand and continues anyway. She says she graduated from
high school in 1944, left Aunt Mildred's house, and went into nurses'
training at a local hospital. As the years went by, she kept up with her
aunt and uncle, telephoning them every few months to let them know
how she was doing. She rarely visited, but when she became engaged to
my father, she called to tell them.

They insisted that the couple come for a Sunday brunch so they
could meet the groom. "When we walked in the door, Aunt Mildred
said, 'I have something for you . . . for your engagement.' She gave me
a box wrapped with a bow," Mom says, shaking her head. "In it was a
wide red leather belt. I remembered it from the days when I lived at the
apartment. It had hung on a hook in Aunt Mildred's closet. It belonged
to her."

"So who paid for the wedding?" I ask, having never thought about this
before. All I know is that they had a large affair at the Belden Stratford
Hotel in Chicago.

"Your dad's parents," she says, as if I should have known. "They paid
for everything . . . even my wedding dress."

She sits quietly for a moment, watching a flight attendant whiz down the aisle of the airplane. Then she folds her napkin neatly and places it on top of the plate of food she didn't eat.

"You know," she says, "those days weren't easy, when I first lived in this country, but on this trip I saw what my life would have been like in Germany."

"How's that?" I say.

"Oh, I don't know." She shrugs her shoulders. "In Germany, their lives seem so small, so narrow. Most of my classmates never traveled, not even outside Stockstadt. The big social event is the grammar-school reunion. Most of the women don't have professions; hardly any of them have had a job. I guess I saw the life I never had. I saw what I might have become.

"You know"—she squints her eyes, as if this makes her see with clarity—"I paid a terrible price . . . for a better life."

In silence, I agree.

Chapter 13

Four months later

Dazed with pain, I try for a moment to remember when it began: hours ago, certainly; maybe yesterday; or is it night now?

All I really know is this feeling, this place where I've been, this terrible state of agony and suspension. Here, endless hours are only long minutes, with no beginning or end; here, the walls moan and howl, everything bound in awful primal shrieks that could come from a dog, a cow, a shifting tectonic plate, or an anguished human.

In a dark corner of this nightmare, I struggle. Curled on a crisply sheeted bed in a dimly lit hospital room, I feel tortured and feverish yet icy in this air, as cold as the blue shadows cast by the streetlights outside.

Hulking machines, with pens and graphs, trace my inner spasms along with the body rhythms of the unborn. Occasionally, some computer erupts in automated beeps; the pens' wild tracks flatten into straight lines, and then a nurse appears, to tug and shake the cords that tether me to reality.

One contraction after another overwhelms me. My limbs twitch and quiver uncontrollably. I feel as battered as an island in a hurricane. I try to remember that I am here for a purpose: the baby, the baby, the baby. But the contractions are my only reality now. I picture myself as one of Picasso's cubist women, all sharp, distorted angles and pursed, dry lips framing gritted teeth, my eyes dark-circled and protruding, each looking in a different direction, like those of a fish. I wish fervently to be anyplace but here, anyone but me.

A new scream startles me, an unfamiliar wail, maybe from my own throat, maybe from someone else, someone in another room, another world. Suddenly, everything is worse. I'm drowning in an undertow of agony, barely conscious, barely here.

White coats appear, enter and leave the room, attend to me. Voices trail; I can't make out what they are saying. Submerged, I wonder whether I will ever break the surface, ever breach my mind's waters again.

Someone is trying to tell me something. At first, I hear the words coming at me as a foreign language, slurred sounds played on the slow speed of a tape player. The tone is imploring, but the meaning is obscure.

Suddenly, the nonsense makes sense. "Let's go have this baby." Here's my mantra: I say the words to myself, over and over, as they tow me in.

I am wheeled on my bed to the delivery room. In a blur, I notice a plastic dish the size of a large casserole, tidily laid with bed linens, a tiny night cap, and a miniature white hospital wrap, sewn closed at the hem. This is what my baby will wear; here is where, in minutes, my baby will lie.

Oxygen tanks, small masks, meters, and tubes wind into the plastic crib in the corner of the room. Panic grips me. Do they think something is wrong with the baby? No, no, they say.

"Are you sure?" I ask again. "What's wrong with the baby?"

"Nothing, nothing," they insist. "It needs to be born."

Blood surges through my veins; my heart is pounding so hard that it bangs against my rib cage and echoes in the remote corners of my body. Maybe my heart, too, is about to be born.

"Push," someone urges impatiently. As if I had a choice, I think with hazy resentment. As if my will, or anything else of me, were still here. Tight in a crouch, I coil up to rally my remaining strength and spring in an explosive heave. Then again. Again, again, again. My face is twisted, wet with tears; my teeth are clenched and my eyes squeezed shut as I rip from me a part of myself.

A piercing sound reverberates, one never heard before—the high-pitched wail of a new life, spontaneous and demanding. The cry is excitement and terror, fury and passion, pain and pleasure, life and death—every note in the octave of human emotion.

I open my eyes. The doctor grasps a ruddy, black-haired, drenched infant, the other survivor of the storm. For the first time our eyes meet, locking onto one another's for life. A long twisted rope, taut and twined in blood, connects me with a baby. A girl.

As soon as she learns the baby has arrived, Mom is at the hospital to see her first granddaughter. She brings me a bouquet of spring flowers and places a box with a pink ribbon on the windowsill.

"How do you feel?" she asks, full of genuine empathy as she bustles into the room.

"Okay," I reply, and then clarify, "pretty good, really."

Mom looks around the room, slips off her jacket, tosses it over the back of a chair. "Is the baby in the nursery?"

"Yes." I sit up and feel with my feet for my slippers. "Let's go see her."

"Let me give you this first." She reaches for the box and hands it to me. Then she sits on the edge of the chair as I pop the ribbon, lift the top off, and unwrap tissue to find a hand-knitted multicolored sweater, booties, and hat.

"Did you make all this?" I ask.

"Yes. I've been working on it a long time. I thought about making it in pink," she smiles. "But then I got superstitious."

"This is perfect," I tell her, holding up the small sweater to admire it. "It's so soft and sweet-looking. Thank you," I say, looking directly at her.

"Let's go see the baby," she says. "I can't wait." Mom takes a few steps, then turns impatiently to wait for me as I slowly, painfully, make my way out of the room and down the hall.

No one is standing in front of the thick picture window where visitors can view the babies in the nursery. We stand together in the center to peer in, but instead I catch our reflection. The last time I noticed that I'm almost a head taller than my mother, we were peering into the display case in Hans's museum, looking at her past. Now, as her eyeglasses glint and reflect the light, we are viewing our future. She cups her hands and presses her nose against the window, just as she did then.

Twelve babies, mostly boys, line the nursery. "She's the third one from the left," I say, pointing to my sleeping infant—the one whose round face is framed by black hair spiking madly from under a pink cap. "Between the two boys."

"Oh," my mother shifts her gaze toward her. "Oh, she's beautiful. Look at all that dark hair." The baby stirs and opens her eyes.

"What color are her eyes?" she asks, straining to see them.

"Sort of a gray-brown," I say. "You know, that murky newborn color." The baby lies still with her eyes wide open for several moments, as if she's examining the tiled ceiling. But she doesn't cry.

"Oh, and she's a good baby," my mother concludes.

"How can you tell?" I ask.

"Well, she's not crying."

"Not now," I reply.

"That's good enough for me," Mom says, gently tapping a finger on the glass to try and get her attention. "There are so many things I want to do with her," she says dreamily, "so many things I want to share."

For a few minutes we stand together in silence, neither of us able to take her eyes off the baby.

"So who does she look like?" I ask at last, breaking away to search my mother's face for an answer. She continues to stare at the baby, but doesn't say anything.

Thinking she didn't hear me, I ask again, "Who does she look like?"

"I don't know," she says.

"Well," I press her, "does she look like me when I was born?"

"I don't know," she says, a little flustered. I . . . I don't remember."

She doesn't remember.

There was a time, before the trip, when this would have both infuriated me and pierced my heart. How could she forget? I'd seethe. So much has been lost in her absorption and denial of the past.

But I saw and heard so much more from her in the hospital—little things, but important ones, hints of what can offset all that she doesn't remember. She said she looks forward to the things she will do with her granddaughter. She knitted her an outfit, just as her Oma Sara would have done. She's happy, just for this moment, that the baby isn't crying. She's living in the present.

With my daughter's birth, my mother and I can begin to re-create a complete set of Matrushka dolls. They may always be disproportionate; some things can never be repaired, some wrongs never righted. But at least—at last—the set is whole.

Chapter 14

Two years after the trip

Tromm
December 27, 1992

Dear Edith,

Today I have sad news. My beloved mother and your dear friend, Mina, died on November 30 in a hospital in Lindenfels. Recently, she had suffered with diabetes, but it was a bad asthma attack that killed her.

She has always been afflicted with the disease. Over the last ten years, it had gotten worse. So many things might trigger an attack. Often, when she spoke or even thought about the past, she would gasp for air.

Last Wednesday, my cousin alarmed me because she could not reach my mother on the phone. (I live in a town about a hundred miles away from my mother's home.) I rang the doctor and he convinced my mother that she needed to go to the hospital.

Worried that her attack was serious, I interrupted my rehearsals at the children's theater where I work. I left immediately to be with her, driving as fast as I could. I made the hour-and-a-half trip in just under an hour. But when I arrived at the hospital, the doctor said that I was too late. She had died a few minutes before I got there.

This was very difficult. I did not get to say goodbye to my mother. I didn't get to comfort her, hold her hand, and give her my love in her last moments.

Now it is Christmas. I'm alone in our house, sorting through her things. It is hard for me. As you know, she saved everything, and I don't know what to keep and what to throw away.

After I found a few things that she saved for you, I decided I must write you. There are some calendars from the 1940s where she marked the dates of the deaths of Herr and Frau Westerfeld. She wrote notes and dates on matchbooks, napkins, and the backs of documents. There are pictures and old letters from you and others who left Germany. When I've found everything of interest to you, I'll send a package.

I found her wallet that she had taken to the hospital. Tucked in the billfold, along with a picture of me, was an old picture of you as a child. Next to it was the last letter you wrote her. I always knew how much she loved you. I think you were very near to her in her last minutes.

Her whole life, she dreamed of seeing you again. Your visit in 1990 made her feel complete. "Now that I have been with Tiddy again," she told me after your trip, "I can die in peace."

I'm disappointed that I never got to see you and my mother together. From my childhood on, she always talked about your family. In fact, she could not stop talking.

I keep many of her stories in my mind. One day, I hope to meet you. We could talk for hours about my mother's life and her close relationship to the Westerfelds.

From my mother's stories, I feel that I've known you for a long time. Your family seems nearer to me than mine. I would be honored if you would come and stay at my house in Tromm.

After all this bad news, I wish you a happy 1993. All the best to your family, especially your daughter, whom my mother spoke of often. She loved her dearly from their one meeting and all the letters she wrote.

> Yours,
> Jürgen,
> Mina's son

Fall 1995: Five years after the trip

A large man—in his fifties, with a fringe of brownish-gray hair skirting his balding head, and piercing blue eyes as unforgettable as his mother's— approaches our little group of six conspicuous Americans in the concourse of the Frankfurt airport.

"Edith? Are you Edith?" he asks my mother in crisp English. Now I notice that he is well dressed in casual clothes, wearing a dark-brown leather jacket with a plaid cashmere scarf.

"Yes." She hesitates, staring up at this towering figure, who could star as Paul Bunyan in one of his own children's theater productions. Mina was very short and slight; it seems impossible this man could be her child.

"Ahhhh, I knew it," he booms joyfully with a wide, toothy grin and outstretched arms. He stoops over to embrace my mother first. "I'm Jürgen," he says as he pats my mother on the back. "You are just as I pictured . . . in many ways, just as my mother described you." He tilts her face gently in his hands so that he can study her features. "I knew you by your dark eyes. So good to see you."

My mother starts to introduce us. "This is my daughter; my son-in-law, Steve; my two grandsons . . ." But before she can finish, Jürgen stretches his arms wider, as if to embrace all of us together, with his arms as well as his words: "I'm so glad you are all here."

Next he greets us one by one, shaking my husband's hand enthusiastically, then each of our sons' hands. When he gets to me, he kisses me on both cheeks, and says, "It's such a pleasure to finally meet you."

Jürgen bends over and squats to look directly into my daughter's eyes. "This must be little Isabelle. Ahhhh, my mother was so pleased to hear when you were born." He takes her hand as she basks in his attention, her large dark eyes beaming at him. "I'm so happy you're here," he bubbles.

Over the past years, Jürgen wrote several letters pleading with us to visit for a week. Finally, when Ingrid Kraft and some of my mother's other classmates telephoned her long-distance, insisting that my mother come to a coffee celebrating a special class reunion, she decided to return to Germany.

But my mother planned for this to be a very different trip from our last. She wanted to get to know Jürgen, let him show us around so that we could see the sites we missed on our last trip. We would go to Stockstadt for the coffee, but mostly we would tour Germany from our home base at Tromm, in what had been Mina's house.

Even before we pull into the driveway at Tromm, we can see that the changes Jürgen has made to his mother's house are striking, even stunning. The collapsed roof on the wing is now repaired, and the exterior of the house has been repainted. The old shutters, the ones with the crescent moons that were a dingy gray and closed tightly, are now wide open and freshly coated in dark green. The outdoor light fixtures gleam with shiny brass, and new shrubs and flower gardens trim the house, giving it a fresh warmth; the place no longer has the neglected, forbidding appearance that it presented in Mina's day.

Inside, the rooms are almost unrecognizable. Jürgen has relocated the front entrance; the place I had hovered when Mina and my mother were reunited is now a wall. When I first walk in, I am completely turned around.

Everything in Mina's dark kitchen is redone. Gone are the newspapers, old furniture, and piles of clothing. Shiny new white appliances, including a microwave, have replaced the 1930s stove and refrigerator. A new dark granite counter and stainless-steel sink, right out of the *Ar-*

chitectural Digest, make it hard to remember the goose-necked pipe and worn porcelain sink that formerly occupied the same space. An expensive antique candelabra hangs where the bare light bulb once dangled over the kitchen table. New large windows and thick white walls, spices, wines, and flowers bring a freshness to the room, so that it feels almost Mediterranean.

All that remains of Mina, I think, are the cats, but they don't lounge on Jürgen's kitchen table. The refinished antique oak rectangle is too nice to serve as their berth. Instead, Jürgen keeps the cats outside. Framing the table are pressed-back chairs; they could be the ones we sat in five years ago, though they've been recaned and refinished.

Here, in the week to come, I'm hoping Jürgen and I will sit and talk for hours, watching the moon rise, sipping German wine, and exploring the places where the streams rushing behind us run parallel.

On our first outing—a walking tour of Stockstadt—Jürgen proves to be an impressive tour guide with a deep knowledge of German history and Stockstadt's culture. He spent years at the university, he says, studying the subjects while trying to understand how and why the Nazi period came about. He has collected all kinds of facts and stories about the town and its role in that era.

"All the names mean something," he says as he takes us down the main street. I look around the street and see that, even in five years, Stockstadt has changed. More people are crowding the streets; new shops have opened, up and down the main street.

"'Stockstadt' means 'town on stilts,'" Jürgen explains. "In the old days, the Rhein would flood, so they built all the buildings on tall sticks.

"Even 'Westerfeld' means something, you know," he continues. "It was customary for Jews to be named after the places they came from. So, for you, Westerfeld is the field in the western parts. Someone in your family must have owned those fields."

As we walk across the street from the liquor-and-magazine kiosk that once was my mother's house, Jürgen says, "This is the house of the Bürgermeister, who I'm sure my mother told you all about."

"Müller?" I ask.

"Yes," he replies with a look of distaste, as if just hearing the name brings a bitterness to his mouth. "Mother never passed up a chance to tell of his bad deeds."

"Yes, we heard all about Müller on our last trip," I answer.

"The next street goes to the church," he continues, gesturing toward the old spire that is captured on my mother's pewter plate.

"This is the Town Hall." Jürgen points to the modern building. "This is the little square where everything happened. Across the street"—Jürgen turns completely around, pointing out a stone archway—"is the pub which they called *Deutsches Haus,* German House. This would be the place where everyone drank."

The place, I think, where my grandfather vowed never to return.

We take a few more steps as Jürgen continues, "At the building next to the pub, the Assembly met." He points to the second floor of the old building. "My mother said that your grandfather Siegmund complained to the Assembly about how he was being treated. The men in the Assembly beat him up and threw him down two flights of stairs, right over there. My mother saw it. She always told me about that incident."

The door to the building's stairwell is propped open so that I can see the steps, the scene of the attack. That makes the event more real to me; in my mind, I place flowers to mark the spot and to memorialize my grandfather. There is no other place of remembrance for him.

But then I recall that on our last trip someone had said that there actually was a grave somewhere for my grandmother. I ask Jürgen about it.

"Yes," he says. "I believe there is a grave for your grandmother in Darmstadt."

"Oh, really," my mother says. Obviously, she knows nothing about this. I wonder if my grandmother's remains are buried there or whether someone just placed the stone to remember her. "Who would have buried her or placed a stone there?"

"I'm not sure," Jürgen says. "Maybe my mother. Would you like to go see it?" he asks my mother directly.

"No," she says adamantly, and then adds in a much softer voice, "That's just not something I . . . I feel I can do."

With that, Jürgen picks up where he left off. "Over there"—he points across the street—"in the house with the little grocery store, lived a guy named Scottie. In fact"—he pauses, rubbing his whiskers—"I think he still lives there. Anyhow, he was also a big Nazi.

"So that gives you some idea of the situation. You see, enemies surrounded your family's house," he says, "like a little country squeezed by superpowers."

"Look here." We walk a little farther up the street. "These big houses belonged to big farms; they had a lot of land. This little street is the Hintergasse, where the socialists and the communists and the workers lived. This is where my grandmother lived."

He points to a small, crumbling old Tudor house, one of the few that haven't been renovated. "You can see," he says, "it's a small house where you couldn't really raise seven children. That's why my grandmother sent my mother to live with your family."

Jürgen points to the road, where cars peel past, screeching and honking their horns. "It's hard to believe it now, when you see this busy street, but my mother always said that the SA came up from Darmstadt and marched here through the main street." In a flash, I can picture the Nazi flags hung from the second stories of the buildings, unfurling in the wind, as women and children lean out the windows to watch the men, a sickening sea of brown jackets, goose-stepping in perfect time.

"See this?" Jürgen says, catapulting me back to 1995. "Nothing is like it was, except this." Jürgen stops and points to a face sculpted high on a stone wall. "This neighbor hates the neighbor across the street. So this is what he did." On the face, the tongue is sticking out of its mouth.

"Look at the neighbor's answer." Directly across the street, at the same point on the wall, is another statement pickaxed in stone. It outlines a person's bare bottom, as if the neighbor is mooning the other.

"Maybe that helps you understand the mentality of this village." Jürgen shakes his head.

"Unadvanced?" I suggest. "Almost medieval, really."

"Yes, and this," Jürgen says, pointing to the bare bottom, "if you can believe it, was the house of the Protestant preacher."

Later, after dinner, the children play outside, chasing the cats and trying to find their secret homes. The adults settle into the kitchen chairs with cups of coffee. As he places a plate of sugar cookies on the table, Jürgen gives us his views on the origins of the war.

Hitler, Jürgen says, brought a kind of prosperity. "That's why there was little resistance in Germany to fight him." He rises to get the coffeepot and refill our cups. "The people were so happy to have jobs that few opposed him. They looked away, figuring: 'It's nothing to us. We are living well. It's better since Hitler is in power.'"

The Nazis, Jürgen says, were masters at marketing themselves and their ideas. They were so persuasive that they even won over many churches. "Many members of the Protestant Church were bitterly anti-Semitic and fervently pro-Nazi," he says. "While the Catholics weren't quite as extreme, the pope supported the Nazis, too."

During the 1936 Olympics, Jürgen explains, Hitler put on a big show in Berlin. The Nazis saw the Olympics as an opportunity to show the whole world how well their political programs worked. For the occasion, they muted their anti-Jewish campaign so as not to frighten or disturb foreign visitors.

"The world thought, 'Yes, they're fighting a bit internally,'" he says, parroting the thinking of the time, "'but it's okay.' Besides, there was a strong Nazi movement in France and Italy."

Even Mina fell to the lure of the Olympics, Jürgen says. She was fond of sports and proud to be in Berlin to watch the Germans win gold medals. At the time, she did not understand that Hitler's propaganda machine was manipulating her and the world.

Jürgen rises, goes over to a shelf, and picks up an old-fashioned 1940s wooden radio with a painted wooden swastika decorating the speaker. "Let me show you something," he says as he holds up the radio. "Hitler mass-produced these and sold them cheap," he explains, "so that he could broadcast his politics and sell himself. Everyone had to have one. It was the only way to keep up with what was going on in the world. Hitler was the first politician in this country to market himself through radio."

"The first master of the new media," I add.

The Nazis were shrewd in other ways, too, Jürgen says. They appropriated many working-class traditions and emblems, organizing marches to honor the nation's workers, opening sports clubs for workers and their families, writing new lyrics about the Third Reich to the familiar tunes of laborers' songs.

"They even took the German word for feeling at home—'*Heimat*,'" Jürgen says, still incredulous at the party's gall. "There is no good translation for that. But this is the word that describes the people, the landscape, the flowers, the meals, the songs, the beer. It is the sense of being at home. The Nazis took that word for their political propaganda. 'We are defending our *Heimat,* or Fatherland, the land of our fathers,' they'd say.

"After the war, no one wanted to use these words." Jürgen shakes his hand to show that the words had become untouchable. "Even now. Without these words, the Germans have felt like they are fatherless . . . and homeless."

After my mother and the children have gone to bed, I ask Jürgen, "Do you feel homeless?" What I'm really trying to fathom is whether he, like me, still lives with the war.

"Most Germans," he says, sweeping his hand through the air, "feel that the war robbed them of a sense of home, culture, and identity. We share a collective guilt, though we weren't responsible for the crimes. We are not proud.

"As schoolchildren, we could never feel pride in who we were. Even now, German high school students envy American students who stand when they play their national anthem at a game." He pauses and then adds, "Some don't even like to admit to being German. When they travel, they call themselves 'Europeans.'"

"But in a way," Jürgen says, pouring sparkling wine into my glass, "I lost more than most." Suddenly, his entire body slumps; dejection sweeps over him. I haven't seen this side of Jürgen; until now, he has seemed jovial and spirited. Whatever he lost plagues him deeply.

"What is it you lost?" I ask. I sense that he and I share something: an unspoken past that gives us kinship; he is a brother in history.

"I . . . I lost my mother," he says, his voice heavy with the weight of his statement. He drops his chin and looks down at his lap. "I lost my mother to the cause," he mumbles.

Have I heard him right?

"Yes." He looks directly at me now. "You see, her failure to save your family consumed her."

Here is a new piece of the puzzle that is my mother's and my past. I think of Mina five years ago, her agitation and hostility, her intensity and passion. Half a century after the Nazis were defeated, Mina had forgotten nothing and forgiven less.

"She was never at peace," Jürgen says. "She never wanted to be at peace." His low voice drops to a whisper. "She became addicted to her cause, never knowing how to . . . how to disengage." He smacks the side of one hand against the palm of the other, indicating a kind of severance or compartmentalization. "It, more than anything else, gave her a reason to live.

"Don't misunderstand me." He raises both hands to clarify, his piercing blue eyes blazing like his mother's. "I'm proud of her, of how she took a position.

"I know I wouldn't want her to be like the others. I was really proud of her," he says as if trying to persuade himself. "It's just . . . It's just . . . that sometimes I wished her principles hadn't tormented her so."

He rubs his thumb along the table, feeling its sharp edge, and then adds, "You know, she could never say: 'This is not my problem. There's nothing I can do about it.' She always felt like . . . like a failure."

"Could she ever get away from it?" I ask. "I mean, was she able to go beyond it, talk about other things and find joy in life?"

"Not really." Jürgen shakes his head several times. "Not really. Oh, she tried. Sometimes she talked and talked about it, and other times, she tried to ignore it all. When I spoke to my stepfather, Paul, about the Third Reich, she would change the subject and say, 'Look how pleasant the birds are.' I would get mad. I'd say, 'Look, Ma, we're talking.' She'd say, 'No, don't talk about this. It makes me nervous.'

"When something came on the television about the Nazis, she would say, 'Please close the door. I don't want to see it.' She would say, 'If I have to look, I'll dream about it again. The whole Westerfeld story will take over my thinking again.'

"She didn't ever want me to ask her questions about the past. She would say, 'I can't stand it.' Suddenly, she would lose her breath and start gasping for air.

"I remember, when I was a child, hearing my mother crying in her bed. At the time, I didn't know what made her so sad. When I was older, she told me she always felt defeated. After the war, Müller was put in jail only for a few days. She had to live with these Nazis' going unpunished."

Mina couldn't accept the fact that after the war nobody remembered anything. She alone couldn't forget. She took it upon herself, Jürgen explains, to redress things in her own way. There was, for example, the grammar-school teacher who had taught Mina. After the war, Jürgen became his student. Mina didn't want him giving her son any second-hand trouble, so she told him: "We both know what you did. You are still a teacher, but if you do any harm to my child, I'll tell the truth about you—that you were one of the strongest Nazis."

"Did that work?" I ask.

"Absolutely," Jürgen says, "After that, he was always correct with me. But these encounters didn't help Mina make friends." In the end, he says, Mina was alone, still at war with everyone around her.

"She couldn't trust anybody," he explains. "Even me. When she got old, she always thought I would sell this house. She thought I would kick her out. She was so withdrawn, so reclusive. When I said, 'Come on, Ma, let me put in central heating, it's too hard for you to gather the wood and coal.' 'No, no, no,' she said." Jürgen changes his voice to imitate Mina's. "'You only want to fix things up so that you can put me out somewhere and you can live here.'

"Then I became angry. I said to her, 'Ma, I've got money. I bought a flat somewhere else just to save on taxes, and here you are living without central heating. I want to help you.'

"'No, no, no,' she'd say, 'leave everything like it is.'"

He picks up the bottle and fills our glasses again, then picks up his own glass to watch the bubbles rise. Slowly he turns its stem in his hand.

"Really, Mother was rare in Stockstadt," he says, still staring at his drink. "She behaved heroically, but she felt like a coward. It turned to hatred."

His temple pulses slightly as he clenches and grinds his teeth. "There's a German word, *atemlos*," he goes on. "That word means 'it takes my breath away' when I think of it." He is speaking slowly now, thinking carefully about what he is saying. "In a way, that was her disease."

In the end, Jürgen says, "*Der Krieg hat ihr den Atem weggenommen*. The war took her breath away."

"It bewildered Mina that Edith could come back here, that she would want to visit or even see her old classmates," Jürgen says as he and I take chairs at the kitchen table the following evening. Again, everyone else has gone to bed, sleeping through our journey into past and present.

"Mina would never have done what Edith has done," he continues. For Mina, he says, in her own words: "'You are a Nazi to the end of your life. You are stamped.'"

"Well," I begin to explain, as Jürgen brings out the glasses and wine, "these trips have been hard for my mother."

"Yes, I can see that." Jürgen uncorks the bottle and places it on the table. "I watch your mother as we talk and she is often biting her lips. She keeps a lot inside." He places a hand on his chest, demonstrating my mother's inner state.

"Still, my mother needed to come back," I say softly. "She left when she was so young. She wanted to restore some of the feeling she had before it was all shattered. She's not a mean or vengeful person. She is a good, generous person who can't do enough, particularly for the people she loves."

"This she shares with Mina," Jürgen says, again taking his seat opposite me and pulling out the next chair so that he can put his feet up on it. "When I was up here, I was not allowed to go to the refrigerator for a snack. She did it. When I got up at five in the morning so that I could make an eight o'clock meeting, she insisted upon getting up to make my breakfast. She even washed and ironed my shirts." It seemed that both Mina and my mother provided for those they loved in ways they themselves had not been provided for, as if they somehow could recover some of what they had lost.

We are silent for a moment, exchanging a lucid gaze of understanding that can rise only from our having both lived in the shadows of the war. Shadows that follow us, darker or lighter, sometimes large and grotesque, sometimes trailing, elongated, into disappearance.

"Nobody came through Nazi Germany pure," Jürgen goes on. "Not even my mother, who did the right thing. She got caught, too." He rearranges his glass on the placemat so that it is perfectly centered.

"It was impossible to behave honorably, have a life, and stay alive," he continues. "I often think of my mother's marriage to my stepfather, Paul. She got to know him in 1933, when he was in the German Army. To her, he was glamorous, and she admired him even in his uniform. She never saw Paul for what he was—a German soldier. If she had, she would've recognized that, as they say, 'All soldiers are potential murderers.' But she didn't want to see that."

Mina was able to rationalize her love for Paul, Jürgen says, and she even felt that marrying him constituted a conspicuous rejection of Nazi Germany. In a way, she was right: Paul was always regarded as different, an anomaly among the tight-knit townspeople, even as a soldier in the Nazi Army. During the war, Paul had been a prisoner of the Americans; later, after the war, he was happy to land a job at the nearby American military base. He worked there most of his life. All of his friends were in the American military, and they often visited Paul and Mina when Jürgen was growing up.

"Still," Jürgen says, "she tried to do something. All Germans had opportunities to prevent all this. Mina knew that how each person behaved in those moments really mattered."

I think of Hans, of his moment of truth. "Do you know Hans Hermann?" I ask.

"Yes. Of course."

"We got to know him on our last trip," I say.

"Then I suppose you saw his museum?"

I nod.

"He is like Mina in that they both must be busy all the time, not to go mad. It's a way of surviving and escaping. Hans collects things, just like my mother did. Both keep everything, because anything could be precious."

Hans, Jürgen explains, ran into trouble with the town officials, who saw promise in his museum and offered financial support, but then told Hans that the museum needed some sort of structure, that he must get rid of some things to make this a useful, educational place for the town. Hans refused, arguing that everything he had was valuable: every Nazi souvenir, every farm utensil, every bone.

"He has no intellectual structure," Jürgen says. "Collecting like this—saving everything—is a form of obsession. I'm sure all this affected his family, too. He probably didn't spend much time with them."

"Oh," I murmur, thinking of Hans's dead son, of a sorrow that can never be eased.

"So you see," Jürgen continues, "nobody walks away from the war. No one came out of this clean. Not even the children. We are never free of it."

While waiting for everyone to get ready to go to the coffee, Jürgen plays with the children in his living room. I hear them giggling and shrieking with delight, sweet piccolos accompanying Jürgen's deep, baritone laugh. When I peek into the room, I see Jürgen taking turns with each child, swinging each by one leg and one arm for an "airplane ride," rattling his lips noisily to imitate the sound of an airplane taking off and landing.

Later, when we have a private moment, Jürgen tells me, "You know, whenever my mother talked about your mother, she always mentioned Edith's deep, dark eyes. She would tell me that they were unlike any she had ever seen; they were beautiful and haunting. It was as if Edith's eyes both captivated and possessed her. When she told me this, I couldn't imagine what it was that moved her so," he says. "Often, I wondered about that. I wished I could see what she was talking about. Now I look into your daughter's deep, dark eyes and I hear my mother's words: 'When I would dream of having children,' she would say, 'I wanted them to have eyes just like Edith's.'

"Your daughter has those eyes," Jürgen whispers. "When I look at her, I truly understand."

The late-afternoon coffee is being held in the same room as the reunion we attended five years ago. As we come through the door, I notice that nothing has changed—the windows, seals on the walls, even the furniture remain exactly as they were.

As we enter the room, several people swarm around my mother with their hands extended to greet her. Hans Hermann darts toward her first, with the same quick movements and crooked smile that I remembered from our last visit. Hans was not my mother's classmate, but when he heard we were returning to Germany, he wrote her that he would come to the coffee.

As he grabs her elbow to hug her, I notice that he looks older now: his creases are deeper and his hair is thinner. After he welcomes my mother and jokes with her, he takes my hand and hugs me. I turn to introduce him to my husband and children, who are standing behind me.

He's particularly thrilled to meet the children, joking and teasing each in a special way. "You are so tall," he says, measuring my elder son's height with a level hand. "Ready to take on your mother, right?"

His eyes light up as I tell him their grade level at school and which sports they play.

"Football or soccer?" he asks my younger son, motioning like a quarterback about to throw a pass and then kicking an imaginary soccer ball with his foot.

"Football," my son replies, and I add "American football," so that Hans understands.

"Ahhhhh," he says, with a wide grin.

"You know"—he turns to me—"I'm hoping to have a grandchild someday soon." When my mother overhears Hans tell me this, she joins our conversation.

"And do you know what I'm hoping my son and his wife will call the child?

"What?" my mother asks.

"Maybe Joshua or Sara," he says poetically. These are the Jewish names some Germans give their children to show their empathy with the Jews who suffered during the Holocaust. He looks to read our reaction.

My mother and I exchange a significant glance, flustered for a moment, neither able to respond to Hans. Finally, I speak for both of us. "We would be honored."

Most of the people who came to the last reunion are here now, though today's coffee is more relaxed, free of the emotional weight of the previous event. Since my mother was honored back then, her classmates talk and behave with great ease around her; she is less an occasion, more a peer. Still, she receives a lot of attention, as many want to tell her about their lives and show her endless pictures of their grandchildren. Others have brought old pictures of the town and the schoolhouse and their class photos to remind them of their times together.

One man points to a sepia photograph of my mother's house and shows it to my son. "This is where we played as children," he says in English, pointing to the space in front of the house.

"Oma, Oma," my son calls out to his grandmother. "What games did you play in front of your house?

"Oma?" he calls again, trying to get his grandmother's attention.

For a moment, the man with the picture looks confused. Then he turns to the man sitting next to him and asks, "*Die Kinder rufen sie 'Oma'?*" I understand what he said: The children call her "Oma"?

"*Ja,*" the man replies. "Isn't that touching? The children call her 'Oma.'"

Epilogue

Shortly after we returned from our first trip, I began to look through the pile of papers Mina had given me. Among them was a program for the graduation exercises at Mount Sinai Hospital School of Nursing in Chicago, held April 17, 1947. It listed the names and hometowns of all forty graduates, including my mother, who surely was proud to be among them and had sent it to Mina. Recognizing that this was a milestone the Westerfelds would have celebrated, Mina had kept the program, in which someone—I wondered whether it had been my mother or Mina—had underlined her name and her hometown: "Edith Westerfeld, Chicago, Illinois."

In the weeks that followed, I slipped back into Mina's papers, a little at a time, savoring each glimpse I took through this new window to the past. Other families have stories, pictures, family legends; I came to consider Mina's papers as my own family chronicle, the "find" from my private archeology. They tell part of my story. They give me the closest thing I will ever have to a family album, my personal archive documenting a newly inherited narrative.

After a while, I realized that I now had a real history and must protect it. So I photocopied everything in the pile, making several copies of each page, although I still had no idea what many of them said. Then I took the pages to a German student at a local college who could translate them into English.

In the pile, I learned, were letters from the Kahns and the Westerfelds, testifying to Mina's integrity and character. She had needed these references to return to Germany after the war. Several legal papers dated 1946 gave Mina the power of attorney to collect the proceeds from the sale of the Westerfeld house. The money was in a bank account frozen during the war; Mina was to receive 25 percent of what it contained. But none of the papers show that she or any Westerfeld ever gained access to the account.

Mina had saved dozens of affidavits and legal documents from January 1948, submitted as evidence in the postwar hearings for the Bürgermeister Müller and the music teacher Peter Schroeder. Several documents established as fact Mina's memory: Müller had ordered Schroeder to stop teaching Betty the mandolin. Mina's carefully folded newspaper clips from the hearings reminded me that they had acquitted both men.

Mina also gave me her personal notes, scribbled in faded ink from a blue fountain pen on frail brown paper, detailing the chronology of what happened to her and the Westerfelds during the 1930s and '40s. She kept her old list of local Nazis, totaling some sixty names. One of them was Albert Lautenschläger, her cousin.

And she saved personal letters from members of Stockstadt's two Jewish families and several from my mother. But the year I was born, Mina and my mother, for one reason or another, stopped exchanging letters. Their correspondence was one of the last threads tying my mother to her childhood. Here is my mother's last letter:

December 27, 1954

Dear Mina,

I wrote you several times and haven't heard back from you. I wonder if my letters reach you. This time, I'll mail this at the post office and hopefully you will receive it.

I hope you are doing well. I was glad to hear that you have remarried. I know that divorcing your first husband was a difficult time for you. He didn't sound like a prize. As dear Oma Sara used to say, "The sky is blue, so what else is new?" There are so many men out there like him.

How old is your son now? I think he is almost 12. Does he go to school in the town? Are the old teachers still there?

Last week, I learned of some very sad news. My mother's sister-in-law, Thea, died in concentration camp. You remember her. She was a very pretty lady who always carried a big purse and brought us candy. Anyway, no one knows what happened to her children.

My dear Mina, you may have already heard that I had a baby girl last month. The stork from the nest in the Rathaus brought her to me. She had to come a long way, but she made it.

She is healthy and active with black hair and very dark brown eyes. My husband is dark like me and a lot of people think we are brother and sister. But we know better, isn't that right, dear Mina?

My child's name is "Fern Brenda." The first name is for our mother, Frieda. The second is for my mother-in-law's mother, Brondl, who died not long ago.

My child was supposed to be born on Dec. 12, so I thought that I had a lot of time before the birth. However, the baby could not wait that long; she wanted to see the world.

Many greetings and kisses to you, your parents, your son, and for the little Edith, dear Mina, who you will have soon.

From your Tiddy

In my home in a suburb of Chicago, there is a display cabinet in the dining room. On the top shelf, I have laid out the tea set Mina gave me, placing it carefully in the same half-circle Mina arranged long ago on her kitchen table. Whenever I catch a glimpse of the china, I am drawn back into Mina's house. I smell the mustiness of the old newspapers and the cats; I see the bare light bulb hanging above the kitchen table, illuminating her whole world. I hear her craggy voice asking me again, "*Willst du sie haben?* Maybe you would like these?"

"Things we have felt with great intensity," Virginia Woolf once wrote, "have an existence independent of our minds; are in fact still in existence. . . ." Those who experienced the war or its half-life know that it lives on; the war's clock has no numbers, no spring, no plug to pull.

In Germany, I saw the intensity of the war's effect on many lives, and how its existence lingers. Those who lived through it have been shaped, then defined, and finally, irreparably damaged by it. Yet they were "the lucky ones," not physically injured by the war, suffering only from its corrosive reach. Mina was one of these, a civilian who resisted heroically and survived. Hans never had a war wound or even the intense guilt of knowing he'd been a Nazi. My mother never endured a concentration camp; she escaped to a new life. All three of these lives were nonetheless warped. Though the children of these victims didn't experience it themselves, they came to know the war intimately. They were born into a world where the war was everyone's overriding legacy.

In my family, the war has devastated three generations. It killed my grandmother, orphaned my mother, robbed me of a mother who could be alive to the present in the only childhood her daughter would have. But it ends here. My daughter will never know the war as a personal history or trauma. For her, the war will be ancient history and family lore, not an open wound.

Now I see that, in many ways, my mother is the hero of this story. It was Hitler's sick dream that no Jewish girl would ever walk the earth again. But that dream is dead; Hitler is dead; and here is my mother, living evidence of his failure. She has entered her eighth decade. She has a family and grandchildren. She lived; she triumphed.

Yet we remain on our own. She and I are muddling through without role models or script, lacking in stories, autobiography, and identity. So much is lost, irretrievable to both of us.

I suppose all families can look back and see such catastrophic times—disasters whose repercussions continue to injure generation after generation. War need not be the source; famine or pogroms abroad, abuse or violence at home all can leave wounds that heal slowly. Any traumatic experience, brutal or subtle, can be perpetuated inadvertently, its damaging effects sometimes smoldering at length before bursting into flame.

In my mother's life, blurred from view by the smoke of huge fires—the loss of her parents, her country, her context—were smaller fires and other losses. Perhaps most disorienting was the lack of witnesses to her childhood; almost no one but Edith remembered young Tiddy. Nobody could share or contradict her childish recollections, provide testimony and a frame of reference.

When we are children, M. R. Montgomery writes, "there is no point in jumping into the swimming pool unless *they* [parents] see you do it. The child crying 'Watch me, watch me,' is not begging for attention; he is pleading for existence itself. *They* will remember. *They* will hold it, keep it, make it true. Everything else is dreams, not memories."

For my mother, going back to Stockstadt was about reclaiming and repossessing some of those memories; it was about damage and repair. For me, it was learning, for the first time, about my mother and her past.

Though she never said it, after we returned from the first trip I came to understand the real reason she decided to visit her place of origin. Her whole life had been shaped, not by the normal human experiences of family and work, but by loss. As the years went by, I think, she began to sense that her loss had become a wedge dividing her from her family—from me. I suppose she feared she might lose me, just as she had lost everyone else she had loved.

Then, somehow, she began to see. She realized that this separation between us was becoming another loss—but one that she could stop. So she took the risky, uncharacteristic step of suggesting that we go to Germany together.

It wasn't something she wanted to do. It wouldn't be easy. But—and as I thought it through, I could almost hear my mother's logic, could see how she had come to this decision and been able to make the trip—

maybe, my mother thought, if I saw where she had come from, if I got a look at her past, I could know something more of who she is and what she lived through. Maybe I would begin to understand. Maybe, if we shared an experience, we could begin to repair.

Almost miraculously, she was right. In the end, the very thing that had pushed us apart now pulled us together: the Motherland, for us a geographic place, and for all mothers and daughters a country of the heart—the one to which we return when, transformed, we ourselves have become the mothers. There, I recovered a few stones from the stream that runs behind me. Now, often, I handle them in my mind, examining their smooth surfaces, searching for secrets, listening for and sometimes hearing the faint trickle of that stream of memory.

Before we made the trip, back into my most distant recollections, my mother's pain was consuming; back then she had not yet forgotten anything, she could not forget, and without forgetting could not be released from the past. Throughout my childhood, she struggled with a pain so great, so distracting and preoccupying, that it obscured the sweetest moments in her life as a mother.

Yet even this might still be repaired. One day recently my mother baby-sat for my children, and when I returned home, she excitedly shared a story.

"I was trying to get Isabelle to bed," she said. "She crawled under the covers, pulled the sheets to her chin, looked up at the ceiling. Absolutely content. Then she said, 'Ohhh, Oma'"—here my mother held her hands under her chin, tugging at an imaginary blanket and giggling—"'Oma, this is the life.'"

I laughed with her, in the way all mothers laugh at the infinite amusement their children provide, and I did not notice my tears until later. They came when I realized that my daughter had reached my mother in a way I never could; that my mother, after a lifetime alone, had at last allowed herself to be touched.

~

When I decided to write this book, I asked my mother, "Do you think you can stand to read it? Or to have others know what happened and how it affected us?"

"Go ahead and do it," she told me without hesitation.

"But will this hurt you?" I asked, concerned that she think it over, that she consider the prospect of seeing her private grief in print.

She thought for a moment. Then she said confidently, "I'm here now."

So I set about the work of sifting through my notes, the letters, the pictures, the tapes—and there I ran into trouble. While listening to some of my conversations with Jürgen, I became frustrated when Isabelle's incessant four-year-old chatter drowned out his words. Over and over, I replayed the same twenty-five second section of the tape, trying to make out what he was saying. But it was impossible; all I could hear was Isabelle's off-key singsong.

I became convinced that those twenty-five seconds contained something crucial. I strained and struggled, listening at a slow speed. At a higher volume. With more bass. I even called an electronics shop, but they couldn't help.

At last, annoyed and discouraged, I set the tape aside.

Then, one day, I listened again, this time changing my focus slightly, as if adjusting the lens of a camera. And I realized that whatever Jürgen was saying in those twenty-five seconds couldn't approach the importance of Isabelle's song, the song of innocence that is childhood, witnessed by her family, and now resonant in our collective memory.

I closed my eyes and listened to nothing but my daughter:

> ". . . *If the looking glass gets broke,*
> *Mama's going to buy you a billy goat.*
> *If that billy goat runs away,*
> *Mama's going to buy you a brand-new day.*"

Acknowledgments

*T*his story has been with me my whole life—continually unfolding and revealing itself with time. It has taken me years, even decades, to gain the insights I've shared here. For the sake of the story, I have telescoped some conversations and events.

Motherland had many midwives. I am indebted to the following people:

My writers' group—Sue Spaeth Cherry, Deborah Leigh Wood, and Michele Blecher—helped conceptualize this book many years ago, and each writer offered me unique feedback during the process. Thanks to all my friends for their support, especially Mary Rose Hamming, Janet Kellogg Petersen, Amy Heber, Renate Staley, Lindy Rubin, and Nan Barrett. Susan Remen King grew up with me and, throughout the years, has helped me to understand. I couldn't have done this work without Jürgen Flügge's cooperation, love, and support. He is like a brother to me.

Thanks to Richard Norton Smith, Terry Zaroff-Evans, and my colleagues at Northwestern University's Medill School of Journalism. I owe a special debt to Thomas Hazlett, who after hearing this story spurred me on by pounding my dining-room table and demanding, "Is there a *writer* in the house?"

My agent, Marian Young, believed in this project, believed in me long before I did. During the writing, she rescued me when I faltered, and through it all, she has become much more than a business associate; she is my friend.

My first editor, Mindy Werner, motivated me with her enthusiasm. My second editor, Kristine Puopolo, greatly improved the manuscript with her invisible hand and sensitive perceptions. And Sarah Baker brought a sense of the possibilities to the final version.

My in-laws, Betty and T. J. Chapman, my stepfather, Larry Breitkopf, and my great-aunt, Anna Smoller, gave me support and encouragement. My paternal grandmother, Gussie Schumer, who died in 1993, gave me the precious love unique to a grandparent. That was its own inspiration.

A special thanks to my father, Dr. William Schumer, for instilling the drive to accomplish, and to my brother and sister-in-law, Scott and Lisa Schumer, for being my booster club.

Though the book took my time and attention away from my children, Ross, Keith, and Isabelle Chapman, I deeply appreciate their love, patience, and tolerance. Maybe *Motherland* will help them to understand.

I am extremely grateful to the people who gave me editorial comments and guidance. When I started the project, Susan Figliulo vowed to sit and watch me write every day so that I could accomplish the task. That wasn't necessary, but she was always there for me and she tidied up my prose with her judicious copyediting. Gail Moss helped me see the arc of the story and talked me through the tough spots. Finally, I feel lucky to be married to Steve Chapman, my first reader and best friend.

FOR THE BEST IN PAPERBACKS, LOOK FOR THE

In every corner of the world, on every subject under the sun, Penguin represents quality and variety—the very best in publishing today.

For complete information about books available from Penguin—including Puffins, Penguin Classics, and Compass—and how to order them, write to us at the appropriate address below. Please note that for copyright reasons the selection of books varies from country to country.

In the United Kingdom: Please write to *Dept. EP, Penguin Books Ltd, Bath Road, Harmondsworth, West Drayton, Middlesex UB7 0DA.*

In the United States: Please write to *Penguin Putnam Inc., P.O. Box 12289 Dept. B, Newark, New Jersey 07101-5289* or call 1-800-788-6262.

In Canada: Please write to *Penguin Books Canada Ltd, 10 Alcorn Avenue, Suite 300, Toronto, Ontario M4V 3B2.*

In Australia: Please write to *Penguin Books Australia Ltd, P.O. Box 257, Ringwood, Victoria 3134.*

In New Zealand: Please write to *Penguin Books (NZ) Ltd, Private Bag 102902, North Shore Mail Centre, Auckland 10.*

In India: Please write to *Penguin Books India Pvt Ltd, 11 Panchsheel Shopping Centre, Panchsheel Park, New Delhi 110 017.*

In the Netherlands: Please write to *Penguin Books Netherlands bv, Postbus 3507, NL-1001 AH Amsterdam.*

In Germany: Please write to *Penguin Books Deutschland GmbH, Metzlerstrasse 26, 60594 Frankfurt am Main.*

In Spain: Please write to *Penguin Books S. A., Bravo Murillo 19, 1° B, 28015 Madrid.*

In Italy: Please write to *Penguin Italia s.r.l., Via Benedetto Croce 2, 20094 Corsico, Milano.*

In France: Please write to *Penguin France, Le Carré Wilson, 62 rue Benjamin Baillaud, 31500 Toulouse.*

In Japan: Please write to *Penguin Books Japan Ltd, Kaneko Building, 2-3-25 Koraku, Bunkyo-Ku, Tokyo 112.*

In South Africa: Please write to *Penguin Books South Africa (Pty) Ltd, Private Bag X14, Parkview, 2122 Johannesburg.*